INDIAN

SILVER

INDIAN SILVER

S.K. PATHAK

Lustre Press
Roli Books

Dedicated to the memory of my parents

ISBN: 978-81-7436-375-6

This edition published by
Roli Books in arrangement with
Roli & Janssen BV, The Netherlands
M-75 Greater Kailash II Market,
New Delhi-110 048, India
Ph: ++91-11-29212782, 29210886
Fax: ++91-11-29217185
E-mail: roli@vsnl.com
Website: rolibooks.com

Text: © S.K. Pathak
Editors: Dipali Singh/Archana Shankar
Design: Arati Subramanyam
Layout: Naresh Mondal
Production: Naresh Nigam; Kumar Raman

Printed and bound in Singapore

Page 1: *A* pichkari *(syringe) used for sprinkling colour during the festival of Holi.*
Page 2: *A silver* jhoola *(swing) used in temples to lull gods to sleep.*
Page 3: *A 19th century* surahi *(wine flask).*
Left and facing page: *A Rajasthani* huqqa *(smoking pipe).*

CONTENTS

INTRODUCTION

One of the earliest metals to have been used by man, not only in India but also in other parts of the world, silver – the brilliant white shining metal – is second only to gold in preciousness. It has carved a special niche for itself due to its malleability and its multiple uses. In India, it perhaps surpasses gold in popularity because of its greater affordability. In fact, most goldsmiths in India craft a variety of silver ornaments, silverware, religious and decorative figures and utility objects. That India has always had a fascination for items such as jewellery, urns, and figures of deities in silver is manifest in palaces, museums, private collections and even in ordinary Indian homes. In the light of studies by scholars on silver jewellery, coins and religious and utility objects, an attempt will be made in this monograph to present an overview of Indian silver.

Silver jewellery dates back to the Harappan period (c. 2500–1800 BC), as evidenced by the excavation of silver objects from the ancient sites of Harappa and Mohenjodaro. Recently, a few damaged silver *churis* (bangles) and some *karas* (thick wire bangles) were found in Maandi (Meerut, Uttar Pradesh), a Harappan site (these are now on display in the National Museum, New Delhi). By the sixth century BC, silver coins known as punch-mark coins were introduced, inaugurating the first coinage in Indian history. Gradually, silver also began to be used to make utility items, as has been corroborated in the findings from excavations at Taxila (early first century of the Christian era), indicating the overall prosperity of the people as well as the popularity of silver as a metal.

Indian coinage is an important source of Indian history. Through the earliest

Facing Page:
Decorative silver piece in the form of a fruit-laden mango tree, on a rounded pedestal, Rajasthan

Below:
Satavahana silver coin of Nahapana, Kshatrapa ruler in Central India, 1st century BC*; both the reverse and obverse sides of this coin, restruck by Gautama Putra Satkarni, are shown here*

Indian punch-mark coins, belonging to the sixth century BC, archaeologists and historians have unravelled many hitherto unknown facts of Indian history. For example, the silver coins used during the Satavahana dynasty – the round shape of the coins, the engraved portraits of kings and queens, their achievements and important events during their rule – constitute a valuable pictorial record of the time. The Satavahanas ruled in the western Deccan in the first century BC but part of their empire was conquered by Nahapana, a powerful Kshatrapa ruler and founder of the Kshatrapa monetary system. He was the first to mint portrait-type silver coins, usually with a thunderbolt and arrow engraved on the reverse.

Each region of India has evolved its own designs and techniques in creating silverware, depending on local traditions, aesthetics and religious beliefs as well as environmental conditions. The state of Kashmir excels in the production of silver plates. These are made in either a shallow repoussé with pierced designs or as flat surfaces with engraved lines. Kashmiri craftsmen make all kinds of functional articles such as tea-sets, trays and jugs. Common designs used are *kalka*, (paisley motifs), the arabesque, the rosette, and *chinar* leaf shapes. Sometimes, silver objects are covered with gold in a technique called the Ganga–Jamuna style.

In Punjab, most silver artefacts are made by Kashmiri workmen who settled there in the nineteenth century, while in Lucknow, from where the erstwhile Nawabs of Awadh once ruled, designs of silver items are similar to Kashmiri workmanship. The silver articles of Lucknow are ornate, with shallow repoussé work depicting hunting scenes or showcasing tree and floral motifs.

The royal families of Rajasthan patronized the manufacturers of silver plates. Known for the fine quality of their creations, Rajasthani artists also crafted exquisite figures of men, women, elephants and camels and fashioned wine flasks, *huqqa*s (smoking pipes) betel-nut boxes, and *itradaan* (scent flagons). Most of these objects can be seen in museums of India, especially the National Museum of New Delhi, which has an impressive

collection of such silver artefacts. Silver images of gods and goddesses, such as Durga, Lakshmi, Ganesha, Krishna, and Saraswati, are popular in India and are kept in tiny shrines in homes for worship. A notable example is a small temple covered with repoussé work that belonged to Gujarati royalty (National Museum).

Cuttack (Orissa), in the eastern part of India, has also produced rich work in silver. Its filigree creations are renowned not only in India, but also all over the world. Artists of this region have produced a large number of decorative items in delicate filigree work, but some artists, however, later moved south to Karimnagar (Andhra Pradesh) and Tiruchipalli (Tamil Nadu), continuing their work there. Filigree work is also created by artists in Central India, Rajasthan and Uttar Pradesh.

Above:
Ornately carved flower basket surrounded by foliage patterns on a silver water pot

Left:
Detail of a foliage design in the cutwork style on a silver box, 20th century, North India

Right:
Latch of a silver box, delicately engraved in high relief, 20th century, Rajasthan

Facing Page:
Silver kalash *(water vessel used for worship) in the shape of a coconut encircled by mango leaves, 20th century, North India*

In Kerala in South India, ornamental and utility articles were made from small silver coins (*chakrama*) threaded together with a fine silver wire or soldered together, leaving small spaces between two pieces to produce the effect of lattice work.

Poona (now Pune, in Maharashtra) and Kutch (Gujarat) were two main centres in western India where silver ornaments and silverware for everyday use were made in a very deep, bold form of repoussé. These creations were often moulded into graceful human shapes or figurines of deities.

With the growing market for modern designs and articles, silver craftsmen need technical knowledge about the amount of alloy required to produce a certain hardness in the metal. In India, large firms, such as the well-known Cooke & Kelvey, have experimented with the quality of alloys and have set their own seal on articles to guarantee the quantity and quality of silver in each piece. Today, Indian craftsmen are second to none in the world in terms of designer and quality silverware, not even to their competitors in European and Arabic countries.

A BRIEF HISTORY OF INDIAN SILVER

Documenting the history and chronology of Indian silver ornaments and artefacts has always been problematic. This is because old ornaments and other silver objects have generally been melted for generations to remake ornaments in newer styles. Further ambiguity was created since there was no system of dating and stamping silver or monitoring the percentage of alloy. Scholars have had to depend on comparative stylistic similarities in art forms of the same period, such as sculptures and paintings, to date silver objects.

The history and chronology of Indian silver and its properties have been traced from the prehistoric period in India. The earliest reference to silverware dates back to the Indus Valley civilization through findings during excavations at various sites, such as Mohenjodaro and Harappa. According to British archeologist, Sir John Marshall, the main discoverer of these sites, silver was more in use here than gold. Silver vessels, beads and a bracelet, along with a cast-silver vase with a lid, containing gold and silver jewellery, have been found in Mohenjodaro.

Silver was used more extensively than gold in India. However, until there is further analysis of the silver objects produced by the people of the Indus Valley, it is not possible to authenticate the source of the silver metal nor the ores used to make it. The silver used in Mohenjodaro, however, was extracted from lead ore, so it is evident that the people of the Indus Valley civilization knew about the technique of casting, in which the shape of an object is moulded in wax and covered with a coat of special clay. Molten silver is then poured in through a hole to melt the wax so that the metal can take its shape. After this, the silver cast is taken out and embellished

Facing Page:
Rare huqqa *base adorned with exquisite* bidri *workmanship, depicting the story of "Padmavat", the 15th century Sufi philosophical work by Malik Muhammad Jayasi, 19th century, North India*

Left:
Delicate net-weaving design work on a silver fan, 20th century, North India

Right:
Fish motifs in a stylized creeper pattern, worked in the repoussé technique on the surface of a silver paandaan *(betel-roll box), 20th century*

with hand tools. They also seemed to have known the technique of raising silver out of a silver sheet, also known as repoussé work, in which the sheet is ornamented in relief by hammering it on the reverse side.

The *Rig Veda* (c. 1500 BC) refers to silver as *rajat*. There are several references to body ornaments in Vedic literature, but not enough material on silver ornaments and the technology used to make them. Several silver punch-mark coins dating from the sixth century BC were discovered during various excavations in India. The earliest coins are irregular in shape and size but later coins were more uniform.

Literary and archaeological sources confirm that India did not lack in metallic wealth or in the art of metal-working since early times. The science of metallurgy was known in India even before the arrival of the Greeks here. Megasthanes, a Greek traveller during the Mauryan period, wrote in his travelogue that "Indian fertile soil had numerous veins of all sorts of metals including silver in no small quantity, which are employed in articles of use as well as the implements and accoutrements of war." Diodorus Siculus, a Greek historian, also confirms these facts.

The import and export of gold and silver objects was also recorded by the classical writers of the time. Herodotus observes that due to the abundance of gold and silver, Indian rulers gave opulent gifts, such as silver rings, bowls and vessels to other kings of Asiatic provinces. This is further substantiated by Kautilya's *Arthashastra*, a treatise on statecraft (4th century BC). From ancient times, India's indigenous sources of silver were negligible. According to some historians, a thousand tons of silver were accumulated through foreign trade in return for Indian spices, cotton, silk, indigo, perfumes and sandalwood. During the Gupta period (AD 312–600) trade through land and sea routes to the East and West increased greatly. The *Jataka Tales* and the *Panchatantra* stories mention that profit in foreign trade increased from 200 to 300 per cent. This trade undoubtedly brought a bulk of silver currency to India.

The Indian Ocean became a major centre of trade between the Chinese, Indians and Arabs. Most of southwest Asia participated in this trade and in return for products such as spices, foreign traders exchanged gold, silver and porcelain. Even during the thirteenth and fourteenth centuries AD, foreign traders coming to the

Left:
Graceful floral design in full relief on a silver pot, North India

Right:
Surface of silver tray embellished with bidri *workmanship in the* chakari *(running wheel) style, Andhra Pradesh*

Below:
Rounded water vessel decorated with ornate depictions of forest and hunting scenes in high relief, Rajasthan

Facing Page:
Exquisite workmanship in the jali *(latticework) style adorns this silver* husnadaan *(vanity box, used to keep perfume or betel-nuts), North India*

Malabar and Cambay regions of India brought silk, gold and silver in exchange for Indian products. Marco Polo has written in his travelogue that he arrived in this region with many ships carrying gold and silver based on the tastes of various patrons.

Ralph Fitch, a European traveller who visited India in the sixteenth century AD, wrote in his memoirs that Indian women were always adorned with silver ornaments. He also mentioned that the Portuguese rulers of India often took as many as 100,000 silver coins from India to trade with China.

The Mughal period was marked by an abundance of silver ornaments and silverware. Thomas Roe, the British ambassador to the court of the Mughal emperor, Jahangir, referred in his memoirs to the trading ship which plied between Surat (Gujarat) and Mecca (Saudi Arabia), bringing large quantities of gold and silver. Through these metals, Indian commodities were purchased from Indian traders. This silver was pure and without any alloy. Jean Baptise Tavernier, a French jeweller who visited India several times during the Mughal period, also referred to the trade of silver between China and India. He has mentioned that silver poured into India not only from China and Japan, but also from Germany, Hungary and pre-Columbus America. François Bernier, a French traveller who visited India during the seventeenth century AD, also wrote in his travelogue that Indian vessels carrying cargo to Burma (now Myanmar), Thailand, Ceylon (now Sri Lanka), Maldives, Mozambique and other countries would bring back precious metals like gold and silver. Silver was amassed in India in this way by traders and used to make silver coins, ornaments, utensils and even furniture. This process continued for many years, and the silver was passed down from generation to generation.

An archaeologist by the name of A. Lucas has pointed out that silver is

Right:
Silver dice and balls used to play the game of chaupar *(an indoor game played in India from ancient times), Rajasthan*

found in nature in three conditions – metallic, non-metallic in ores or combined with gold. The metallic form is not likely to have been the source of silver used at Mohenjodaro, because it was as rare in ancient times as it is now.

Silver is commonly found in the form of sulphide or chloride, mixed with other metals, such as lead, zinc or copper. A certain amount of expertise is necessary to reduce it to its metallic state. Silver frequently occurs in small quantities together with lead as argentiferous galena. Lead was by no means rare in Mohenjodaro and it is possible that silver was extracted from the ore of lead. Both pure and combined silver are much too soft, and it is difficult to mould any shapes from either of them. Depending on the nature of the objects, silversmiths would alloy the silver with copper or other metals, in accordance with the proportional requirement.

Generally, silver is purchased and processed in the form of *silli* (a lump in the shape of a brick). In India, pure silver is called *tejabi chandi* (acid silver). To alloy silver with copper, silver is placed in a clay bowl or iron container, along with the required copper, and heated. While heating both, borax is mixed thoroughly with silver until it is assimilated. Through this process,

50 per cent copper can be alloyed with silver and helps to harden it. The silver can then be fashioned into ornaments and other objects that need fastening. For chisel work, pure silver is required, but silver bangles or rings are usually made of silver alloyed with copper. The trained eye of the silversmith or other professionals can detect the proportion of silver with copper from the marking on a touchstone. Pure silver marking would be much whiter than the copper alloy, which looks duller. Gold and silver alloyed pieces can also be separated – alloyed pieces are put into acid, which makes the gold soft like clay, while silver is reduced to a liquid form. This portion of liquid is mixed with four portions of water – copper is placed into the solution, so that silver clings to it. Then the material becomes malleable enough to be shaped into various objects.

Below:
Chaupar *board with dice and balls; the cotton cloth base is ornamented with* zari *(silver thread) workmanship in relief, Gujarat*

TECHNICAL KNOWHOW

The origin of the word 'metal' can be traced back to meteorites, considered sacred by Indians. The shaping of metal was a secret ritual and the blacksmith's forge was sacrosanct. Indian craftsmen treated their tools and ornaments as gods, venerating them before starting a new day of work. The tools were dedicated to Lord Vishvakarma – most Hindu artisans are disciples of this deity, architect of the Hindu gods and the master of all craftsmen.

The princely families of India commissioned artisans to make silver and enamelled jewellery as well as silver items, such as sword handles and utensils. Horse and elephant trappings too were sometimes made in silver and studded with gems. Today, more modest silver objects, generally plain and easy to maintain, are in demand. If these are to be embellished, goldsmiths avoid dirt-gathering encrustations and work on flat, easy-to-clean surfaces.

Various techniques, including round carving, etching, encrustation, filigree and repoussé were used in the creation of silver objects. The plain surfaces of these items were carved, sometimes accompanied by surface ornamentation, such as enamelling, *bidri* and *swamy* work, to add value to the object, depending on the tastes of the clients. Some important techniques of crafting silver will now be briefly discussed to give an idea of the rich tradition of silver and the making of silver objects in India.

REPOUSSÉ

Repoussé is a technique which involves shaping or embellishing articles with patterns in relief, made by hammering or indentation on the reverse side. The silver is usually oxidized. The object is made of

Facing Page: *Ornate filigree workmanship on a silver box skirted with rows of tiny bells, Karimnagar, Andhra Pradesh*

carved wood over which a thin silver plate is hammered, so that it takes the shape of the woodcarving. This technique differs from region to region. It is believed that as a result of the Dutch influence on Indian silverware, shallow-repoussé articles were also produced. In the Kutch region of Gujarat, where the silver bar is used, the repoussé ornamentation is much shallower than that of the South, where the design is raised high in relief. Repoussé work generally consists of an intricate floral design, in a style that is peculiar to the place where it is done. The effect is of white, frosted silver with a bright raised surface and burnished bases.

In most parts of India, repoussé work is carried out by punching in the material's surface to make a depression. Before the background is depressed to raise the design, the vessel is filled with *kil* (a slightly elastic medium of wax and resin). After the main work is done, the vessel is emptied, cleaned, heated and refilled. The *kil* is again melted and removed and the vessel is burnished and frosted. The background is then punched in with the help of steel tools with blunt ends to produce the design in repoussé. The final frosting is done by heating the article and dipping it into a weak solution of nitric acid and water. After this process, the silversmith applies finishing touches, such as polishing with a corundum-like powder called *sangbari reti*. For a glossy appearance, the surface is polished with needles and beads made of steel.

The repoussé work done in Pune is bold and raised, but in Baroda, the object is made of carved wood over which a thin layer of silver is laid and gently and skilfully hammered till the metal takes the shape of the woodcarving. The repoussé work of Kolkata is also of a different style. The designs generally comprise of hunting and forest scenes and rural landscapes. These are worked on frosted silver surfaces, which produce a muted yet rich effect. This kind of work is very popular all over India.

In South India, repoussé work is also carried out on silver. The article is first filled with a composite of gum, sandarac, brick dust and oil, and then heated to melt the silver. Once it cools, the composite becomes hard, like sealing wax. The surface of the vessel is then

Facing Page: *Oval silver tray ornamented with a depiction in high relief of the disrobing of Draupadi, wife of the Pandavas, 19th century, North India*

Below:
Detail of silver tray on facing page, showing the canopied throne in the Kaurava royal court

Facing Page:
Silver box (used to keep scent bottles) embellished with fine filigreed flower and bud designs on the roundels, 19th century, Andhra Pradesh

Left:
Detail of exquisite filigree work on the silver box, 19th century, Karimnagar, Andhra Pradesh

Right:
Detail of leaf and floral designs in fine filigree workmanship on a silver gulab-pash *(rosewater sprinkler), North India*

smeared with chalk, mixed with water and the design is carefully drawn on it with a sharp stylus. The ornament is raised above the surface by beating down the part between the figure and design with steel tools and a hammer. When the object has been roughly embossed, the composite is heated

again and poured out. The unwanted depressions on the surface of the object are corrected and the decorative details and embellishments are added with the use of smaller and finer tools.

FILIGREE

Filigree is one of the finest techniques of crafting silver jewellery and other objects. Filigreed articles are usually made of very thin silver but they are sometimes made in gold as well. This craft is practised

today in mainly three centres in India – Cuttack in Orissa, Karimnagar in Andhra Pradesh and Murshidabad in West Bengal. The raw material used in filigree work is pure silver wire that is bent into

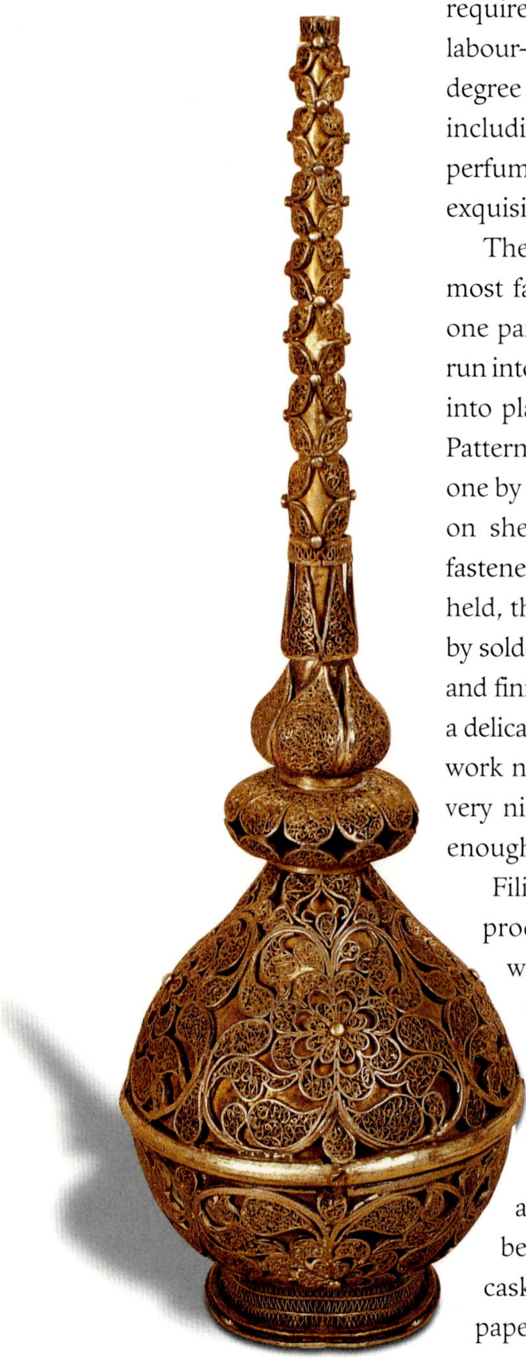

required shapes. The procedure is very labour-intensive and requires a very high degree of dexterity. A variety of articles, including models of birds and flowers, perfume bottles, cigarette boxes and exquisite jewellery are made in filigree.

The filigree work of Cuttack is the most famous. Made of pure silver with one part lead, it is first cast into bars to run into moulds. The silver is then beaten into plates which are drawn into wires. Patterns are formed by taking the wires one by one and carefully arranging them on sheets of mica on which they are fastened by a particular cement. Thus held, the different parts are then united by soldering. The article is finally cleaned and finished, giving Cuttack filigree work a delicate and frosted appearance. Filigree work needs to be done by workers with very nimble fingers and eyesight sharp enough to do this intricate work.

Filigree work of high quality is also produced in Dhaka, Bangladesh, where the technique is very similar to that of Cuttack. Karimnagar district is another centre known for fine filigree work of exquisite workmanship. The finest silver thread is used to evolve unique articles, such as ashtrays, bangles, betel-nut boxes, brooches, buttons, caskets, cigarette cases, flower vases, paper-cutters and photo-frames.

Some of the tools used by filigree workers are *siari* (large pincer), *kalam* (punch), *katani* (wire-nipper/cutter), *sala* (engraver), *charakhi* (a wooden winder), *balancha* (a brush made of hog hair), *meghnala* (mica plate) *tara gola nail* (cylinder made of wood), *hatal* (fine iron needle) and *jantri* (wire-drawer plate made of steel). Similar tools are used all over the country, but the names vary, depending on the language spoken.

SWAMY WORK

Swamy work is usually executed on gold and silver. This technique, really a kind of repoussé work, is used to produce raised figures of gods and goddesses on medallions and canopied niches. The figures can be beaten out from the metal surface of the article, or they are made separately and then skilfully rivetted or soldered onto the article. The best *swamy* work is done in Tanjore, in South India. There are three kinds of this work: brass engraved, brass encrusted with copper and copper encrusted with silver. The encrusting of copperware with silver figures is a modern adaptation of the traditional art of covering brass with copper figures, after which silver is attached to copper or brass.

BIDRI

Damascening in silver on metal alloy is called *bidri*ware This name has been derived from Bidar, in the erstwhile state of Hyderabad, now in Karnataka. Muslim craftsmen of Bidar specialize in making *bidri*ware, using a technique in which a rough cast of the artefact to be made is first obtained. This is done by covering a mould with a mixture of resin and wax. The resin is required to harden the wax. Over this is placed a coating of red clay, supported by stops, over which molten wax and metal are poured. When the roughly cast article is ready, it is placed on a lathe. The design is then drawn and cut out with a fine pointed instrument. Pure silver sheets or wires are inlaid onto the design and the article is again filled and polished, after which it is cleaned with soil containing saltpetre. The raw material used in making *bidri*ware includes zinc, copper, pure silver and small quantities of saltpetre, copper sulphite and salt ammoniac.

Facing Page:
Graceful gulab-pash *(rosewater sprinkler) ornamented with beautiful floral motifs in filigree work, 19th century, East India*

Above:
Floral and leaf designs in rich red and blue on a silver plate, 20th century, North India

Age-old Craft

In ancient times, Bidar was an important seat of a Hindu kingdom of the same name. It is commonly believed that a Hindu king of Bidar invented the craft of bidriware *and used ornate articles to hold flowers and other offerings in honour of household deities. After its conquest by Muslim invaders, Bidar continued to be the seat of government of the Bahmani dynasty of Muslim rulers. The quality of* bidriware *improved and reached its zenith under the patronage of the Muslim sovereigns, who strengthened the craft, encouraging and supporting local artisans.*

The alloy used in bidri *varied from place to place according to the availability of material and local techniques. A chemical solution of copper caliphate, salt ammoniac, common salt and caliphate are applied to the surface of the vessel to be decorated. The chemical turns the metal jet-black. The design is then engraved on the blackened*

***Left:** A variety of floral motifs exemplifying* bidriware *workmanship, 20th century, South India*

surface with a steel engraver. The pattern is then carefully grooved with fine chisels and the precise use of delicate hammers. The fine silver wire is hammered to form an integral whole and the last stage consists of polishing so that the silver design stands out against the black surface.

There are two types of bidri *work:* teh nishan, *in which the design is deeply cut, and* zar nishan *or* zar buland *which resembles the encrusted silverware of Tanjore. In the* zar nishan *type of*

Right: *Parts of a box, displaying* bidri *workmanship – a floral design on the lid (top),the lower part of the box covered with Koranic verses in fine calligraphy (centre) and a close-up of the calligraphy (bottom), 20th century, South India*

work, the design is engraved, after which silver leaves are placed on the surface and rubbed with thin silver foil. This is cut out into the design shape. The edges of each silver leaf are bent over and the depression which ensues is filled with soft lead. The pieces are pressed into the engraved outlines and the carved designs are gently hammered and punched all

***Above:** Photo-frames in silver* bidri *work encasing portraits of Mumtaz Mahal and Mughal emperor Shah Jahan;*
***Below:** Silver elephant with a raised trunk and an ornamented seat on the back, 20th century, South India*

around till the applied decoration is fixed to the base metal.

Between the eighteenth and nineteenth centuries, bidriware *held a special significance in the Hyderabad region. No dowry was considered complete unless a full set of* bidriware *was included. In order to fulfill this requirement, middle-class families began to collect* bidriware *long before their daughters reached a marriageable age.*

Today, Lucknow (Uttar Pradesh), Purniah (Bihar), Tiruchirapalli (Tamil Nadu) and Murshidabad (West Bengal) specialize in making bidriware. *Its fame has spread abroad with the increase in tourism and many items, blending traditional and modern styles, are produced today for sale to tourists. These include boxes of all kinds, bookends, tea-pots, cigarette cases, ashtrays, fruit dishes, cake stands, jewellery and ornaments.*

***Right:** Delicately embellished water pot with overall* buti *(small flowers) design in* bidriware, *20th century, South India*

Facing Page:
Huqqa *base (smoking pipe container) ornamented with deeply etched enamelling work depicting peacocks and other birds, flowers and architectural silhouettes, South India.*

Left:
Detail of the huqqa *base, showing damascening craftsmanship*

Right:
Detail of enamelling work on huqqa *base*

DAMASCENING AND ENCRUSTING TECHNIQUE

Both the terms 'damascening' and 'encrusting', denote the surface ornamentation of one metal by the application of one or more metals. Practically, damascening involves encrusting gold and sometimes silver wires on metal surfaces. Designs are chased on the base metal surface with a very hard and sharp stylus, and a gold or silver wire is hammered into the grooves until it unites with the surface metal. One metal, in the form of wire, is encrusted into another, producing a beautiful and harmonious effect. The two metals, the base of steel, iron or bronze, and the ornamental design in either gold or silver wire form an integral whole after damascening work.

The term 'damascening' is derived from the name of the place where this technique originated – Damascus, Syria. In the Indian subcontinent, this type of work is done in Jaipur, Alwar, Travancore, Kashmir, Bidar and in Sialkot (now in Pakistan). The articles, techniques and designs differ from place to place, varying with the local environment, traditions

and culture. Also known as *koftagiri* work, this technique is believed to have started in ancient Damascus and reached India during the Mughal period, probably via Iran and Afghanistan.

Earlier damascening work was ornamental and was used to decorate weapons like daggers and swords. The Mughal emperor Akbar is said to have been so fascinated by this art that he personally supervised the work in his royal armoury. More recently, this technique has been used to embellish jewellery and other boxes, betel-nut cutters, *huqqa* bases, pitchers, trays and other articles of daily use.

Below:
Mango-shaped silver box decorated with floral motifs executed in the encrustation technique, 20th century, North India

Facing Page:
Silver box richly ornamented with foliage patterns in damascening and encrustation workmanship, North India

Damascening or *koftagiri* work involves first drawing patterns on a steel surface with a hard steel needle or *silai*. This leaves a line that is sufficiently deep to hold the very fine wire that is laid on the surface. The silver wire is drawn through a steel *jandri* and hammered into the pattern. It is then heated and hammered again. Afterwards, the surface is polished with pure white stone.

The techniques of damascening differs in various parts of the country. The following styles are practised in India:

Teh nishan or true damascening;
Shallow *koftagiri*
Dewali work or imitation *koftagiri*
Ganga–Jamuna work

In *teh nishan*, the base metal of steel is engraved very deeply and thick silver wires are hammered into the chasing while the metal is still hot. It is filled again, cleaned and glued until its surface

Right:
An enamelled rich purple and golden-polished floral design in the Muslim style covers the surface of this elegant gulab-pash *(rosewater sprinkler), 20th century, North India*

becomes smooth and polished. No chemical is used during this process.

In the second process of *koftagiri,* a shallow chasing is carried out, after which the wire is embedded in the chasing. Only a thin silver wire can be laid in the shallow grooves, so the surface cannot be polished a great deal.

The third process, *dewali* work, involves the base metal being smoothened with a pumice stone and the pattern etched on it with a stylus. Then it is heated and a silver leaf is applied to it. In the finishing process, the metal is gently rubbed and hammered with a special stone to give the silver a polished look.

In the Ganga–Jamuna, style, the same process that is used in true damascening is employed, but with the use of gold and silver wires in the damascening workmanship.

In Tanjore silverware, the metal is repousséd by working it over a bed of lac. This is laid on the surface of the base metal upon which it is to be joined, and then deeply chased. This technique ensures that the grooved outline can accommodate the edge of the applied ornament with a harmonious effect.

ENAMELLING

Enamelling is the art of colouring as well as embellishing the surface of metal by fusing together various mineral substances. The various regions in India specialize in different designs and techniques of enamelling but the basic process is the same everywhere. The designs are first prepared by a *chitera* (artist), after which the article to be enamelled is made and passed to the *gherai* (the chaser or engraver) who engraves the pattern. The *meenakar* (enameller) then applies the colour in the order of hardness or resistance to the heat of fire. For embellishing silver ornaments, only black, green, blue, dark yellow, orange, pink and a peculiar salmon colour can be used. For polishing the objects, different techniques are used by silversmiths in various parts of India.

Left:
Details of the fine enamelling work on the rosewater sprinkler on the facing page.

The art of enamelling or *meenakari* on metal was well known in ancient India and practised throughout India during the mediaeval period. Today, the *meenakari* work of Alwar and Jaipur in Rajasthan, Lucknow and Varanasi in Uttar Pradesh, Delhi and Kashmir are famous.

The method of enamelling employed in India is called the champlevé. In this process, the metal is engraved or chased to provide the necessary depressions in which the enamel colours are applied and heated. The article to be enamelled is first burnished to a fine lustre. The colours are applied in order of their fusibility – those requiring the most heat are used first. After each colour is embedded in the engraved lines, the object is exposed to fire. When all the colours are applied, the article is finely polished with corundum and cleaned in strong acid. The engraving tools are made of steel and polished with agate tools. Before enamelling, the ornament's surface should be fully burnished and cleaned.

In enamel work, there are slight variations in the techniques employed in

Below:
Side view of a silver box, showing the perfect symmetry of the floral design on the border in high relief, 20th century, North India

Facing Page:
Lid of the silver box (shown below) depicting Lord Vishnu seated with goddess Lakshmi on a bed of cobras and flanked by two trees, in high relief, 20th century, North India

various parts of India. In Kashmir, the article is repousséd before enamelling, whereas in Delhi, Varanasi, Lucknow and Jaipur, the surface is first engraved or chased. Craftsmen of Lucknow and Rampur produce articles with etched designs on silver in which blue and green enamelling is prominent.

In Varanasi, the style is called *gulabi meena* (pink enamel), with at least five different enamel applications and firing of the object to fuse the enamel to the silver. The background colour and the design itself is produced with precious and semi-precious stones, set in enamel.

Apart from these techniques, there is a plethora of regional variations used by silversmiths for making and ornamenting silver objects. These are made according to the wishes of patrons, designers and the market as well as personal designs created by the silversmith who can mould silver, a versatile medium, into various shapes. The National Museum, New Delhi, has some objects on display, which are excellent examples of such work – an enamelled mango tree, a wine bottle that looks like a doll and a *huqqa* in the shape of a woman. These unique objects exemplify the world of silver as a mix of tradition and innovation.

The craftsmen who create the widearray of silver objects are traditionally presumed to be the descendents of their divine ancestor, the ace craftsman Lord Vishvakarma. In the same way as most handicrafts of India, the art and secrets of these techniques are handed down from generation to generation, changing to meet the requirements of modern fashion, but always remaining firmly entrenched in tradition.

SILVER JEWELLERY IN INDIA

Jewellery originated from the innate desire of human beings for adornment. People in ancient times used flowers, leaves, feathers and stones as embellishment and even today, in some tribal societies, women use various objects as ornaments, such as feathers, cowries, seeds and even wings of insects. Later, the shapes and designs of these forms were recreated in gold and silver by jewellers.

Indian jewellery has existed in almost an unchanged form through the centuries, its tradition handed down from the ancient epics, the Ramayana and Mahabharata. The *Rig Veda*, *Sama Veda*, *Yajur Veda* and *Atharva Veda* also refer to the use of jewellery. Each object used in society was representative of the status of the wearer and was believed to have been imbued with magical properties. In tribal society, *tabeej*, an amulet which has prayers inscribed on it, is said to protect the wearer from evil influences, as is jewellery inscribed with figures of local deities. Traditionally, jewellery was (and still is) mandatory for Indian married women who were not expected to be seen without a necklace, earrings, head ornaments and bangles. A widow was not supposed to wear the jewellery of a married woman as it was considered inauspicious.

Each region of India has distinctive styles of jewellery specific to it. Many factors – castes, cultural developments, external influences such as those from migratory tribes and trade contacts – influence the styles of a particular place. If we consider the nose ornament, for example, there was – surprisingly – hardly any reference to it in early Indian literature, sculptures or murals. The earliest depiction of the nose ornament is from the tenth century AD, in Mughal miniature and Rajasthani paintings. This has led to the

Facing Page:
Silver hansuli *(neck ornament), with snake-shaped hooks; finely ornamented with geometrical patterns in the centre and enhanced by transverse lines, 20th century, eastern India*

Below:
Part of a silver bracelet, with clasp, ringed by rounded buds, 20th century

inference that the nose ornament was introduced in India only after the invasion of the Arabs in the ninth–tenth century AD.

Excavations at the Indus Valley civilization sites of Mohenjodaro and Harappa (now in Pakistan), Mehargarh (Pakistan), Kalibangan (Rajasthan), Dhoulavira (Gujarat) and Kunal (Haryana) have uncovered several beads in a variety of shapes and materials, including silver, which was used to make necklaces and hand ornaments. The earliest evidence of silver jewellery has been from the Indus Valley – silver strips found in Kunal may have been used in tiaras in the early Harappan phase of the Indus civilization.

Some silver utensils and gold jewellery have been found in excavations from Taxila (now in Pakistan). These ornaments reveal fine workmanship (some designs and shapes are still replicated in modern jewellery). Few jewellery pieces have been found from the later period, but several stone, terracotta and bronze sculptures, especially of the female form, throughout Indian history have depicted a range of jewellery, showing some exquisitely designed pieces that have ornamented some early female clay figurines from the Mauryan (third century BC) and Sunga (second century BC) periods. Stone sculptures from the Gupta (fourth–fifth century AD), Pratihara (seventh–ninth century AD), and Pala (ninth–twelfth century AD) periods and bronzes from the Chola (tenth–eleventh century AD) and Nayak (twelfth–thirteenth century) periods, apart from mural paintings of Ajanta and Ellora, and miniature paintings of the mediaeval period, tell of the rich unbroken jewellery tradition that existed all over India. Lavish care was taken on the ornamentation of the body, from head to toe, and the study of ancient Indian antiquities reveals that not only women but men also decorated themselves with different kinds of ornaments. The neck was adorned with a complex array of necklaces and chokers, accompanied by chains hanging down to the waist. The ears were covered with earrings and the wrists and arms with bangles, bracelets and armlets of various designs.

The Ramayana mentions that not only Sita, but her husband Rama also wore ornaments made of different materials. In the Mahabharata too, princes Arjuna, Yudhishtra and other royalty wore jewellery. The practice of wearing ornaments – necklaces, armlets, rings and crown – is still observed by most of the

royals of India, although this is now restricted to a few special occasions like weddings or festivals. Sir Thomas Roe, who visited India during Jahangir's time (1558–1605), has described Jahangir's ornaments in detail. Jahangir had a special fascination for jade, but the detail on his ornaments were also executed in silver and gold. The chronicles and autobiographies of Mughal rulers and accounts of travels

Above:
Hand ornaments – bangles, bracelets, and rings – in silver on a woman's hands and wrists, 20th century, Rajasthan

Above:
Silver necklace, studded with semi-precious stones and centred by an ornately engraved pendant, 20th century, Rajasthan

by the Europeans who travelled during the period, describe the jewellery worn by the emperor and empress. *Ain-i-Akbari*, by Abul Fazl of Mughal emperor Akbar's court, refers to ornaments for various parts of the body and further describes the handiwork of numerous people in making and storing these items. Jahangir, Shah Jahan and Aurangzeb were also fond of jewellery and these valuables were part of the *khilwat* (gifts from Mughal emperors to courtesans, according to their status). Bernier, who was in India in 1658–59, has recorded that: "The Indians make excellent pieces and such beautiful ornaments that it may be doubted if the exquisite workmanship of these articles can be exceeded by any European goldsmith." He also notes that: "The empire was an abyss of gold and silver, in the first place, because so much was melted and wasted in fabricating women's bracelets both for the hands and feet, charms, earrings, nose and finger rings and a still larger quantity is consumed in embroidery work on gold and silver clothes, brocades, etc ... the quantity of these articles made in India is incredible."

During the last days of Mughal rule and after the advent of the British, the use of silver ornaments became popular. An interesting reference is from the travel account of Lady Nugent, wife of Sir G. Nugent, Commander-in-Chief (1811–1813) of the army. She describes her visit to the widow of Nawab Mir Jafar, who wore magnificent jewellery even at the age of ninety-six. The old lady delighted her visitor by presenting her with half a dozen necklaces composed of silver fruit and flowers.

Silver jewellery has been in use among tribals and the less affluent sections of Indian society but it became even more popular after the arrival of Muslims in India. Banjara (a nomadic tribe) women are perhaps the most heavily ornamented in the world; their gorgeous costumes, sometimes studded with mirrors and striking embellishments, are an external manifestation of their great zest for life. These ornaments are made of silver and are usually chunky, but also include delicate chains, which are placed on the hair and face. Banjara women always carry at least twelve pounds of ornaments, be it earrings, necklaces or waist-bands, on themselves.

Amulets are also worn as ornaments, used to ward off evil spirits. In some communities when a man remarries, the second wife wears a gold or silver plate with an image of the dead wife on it, so that she is not tormented by the spirit of her predecessor. It was the practice to give a silver ornament with a gold plate engraved with the image of the goddess of smallpox, Sitla Devi, to a child after an attack of the disease to prevent its recurrence. A child recovering from sore eyes is a cue to make an offering of a silver eye to the Devi. Six days after a child is born, strings of black thread or chains of gold or silver, depending on the parents' means, are tied round the hands, feet and stomach of a child to ensure protection from illness or danger.

Many primitive tribes dwell in India and live close to nature, in forests or mountains, and have their own ideas of beauty and adornment. Some tribals in North India and especially in Orissa, decorate themselves with more flowers than clothes. Most of India's tribal belt is concentrated around Gujarat, Rajasthan, Madhya Pradesh, and Orissa where silver ornaments, made by local silversmiths, are greatly favoured.

The tribals of South India also have a pronounced interest in decorating themselves with jewellery. In Kerala, inhabitants of the Attapadi region have a distinctive way of adorning themselves. Since their economic condition does not allow them to wear gold, silver is worn, although not in large amounts. One of the most important ornaments for the women of the Mudgar and Irula tribes of Kerala is a necklace of silver coins and it is the desire of every woman to have at least one of these ornaments. It is also the aspiration of most men to present at least one necklace made of silver coins of four-anna, eight-anna, or one-rupee denominations to their brides after marriage. They use British colonial silver coins, strung together to make the necklace, in the belief that these are pure silver.

Below:
Chunky silver bracelet with triangular openings and floral designs, 20th century, North India

Facing Page:
Full view of silver braid ornament for the hair, festooned with cylindrical pendants and embellished with conical and pellet bells, 20th century, North India

Below:
Part of the tasselled braid ornament on facing page

Before studying the types of silver jewellery in India, we should know something about the craftsmen who make silver ornaments and other decorative objects. Hinduism classifies its people into four main castes (*varnas*):

[1] Brahmins: The priestly Brahmins practised rituals and religious teachings in society.
[2] Kshatriyas: The warriors, they ruled and defended the state and people from enemies.
[3] Vaishyas: The traders and businessmen, they were the backbone of the state and society.
[4] Shudras: The fourth category, they were workers or labourers.

In ancient times, every person was bound by the hereditary occupation of their class, a norm less strictly adhered to now. A person who makes jewellery is called a *sonar* or *swarnkar* (goldsmith) in North India. These goldsmiths also made silver jewellery. Although silversmiths are traditionally Vaishyas (businessman), silversmiths have attempted to pass off as Brahmins or Rajputs in some parts of India. Most North Indian silversmiths are followers of the gods Shiva and Vishnu, but both also have an abiding faith in Vishvakarma, the supreme god of artisans. They start their work after paying obeisance to their furnace, tools, and working place so that it may bring them success and prosperity. On the day dedicated to honouring Vishvakarma, silversmiths all over India worship their implements and will not work with their tools on that day. In South India, the artisans are known as *kammalans* – they have attempted to Brahminize themselves to upgrade their status in the caste system.

TECHNIQUE OF SILVER WORKING

Pure silver is too soft to withstand hammering. To provide it with more strength, it is generally alloyed with copper. The proportion differs according to the requirements of the objects that are to be made. Silversmiths have been important members of village communities from time immemorial. Besides silver, they make ornaments of a variety of materials, including lac and glass, and are either plain or studded with pearls, diamonds and other gems. These are used as ornaments to adorn the following parts of the body:

Head and forehead
Nose and ears
Neck
Arms and hands
Waist
Ankles and toes

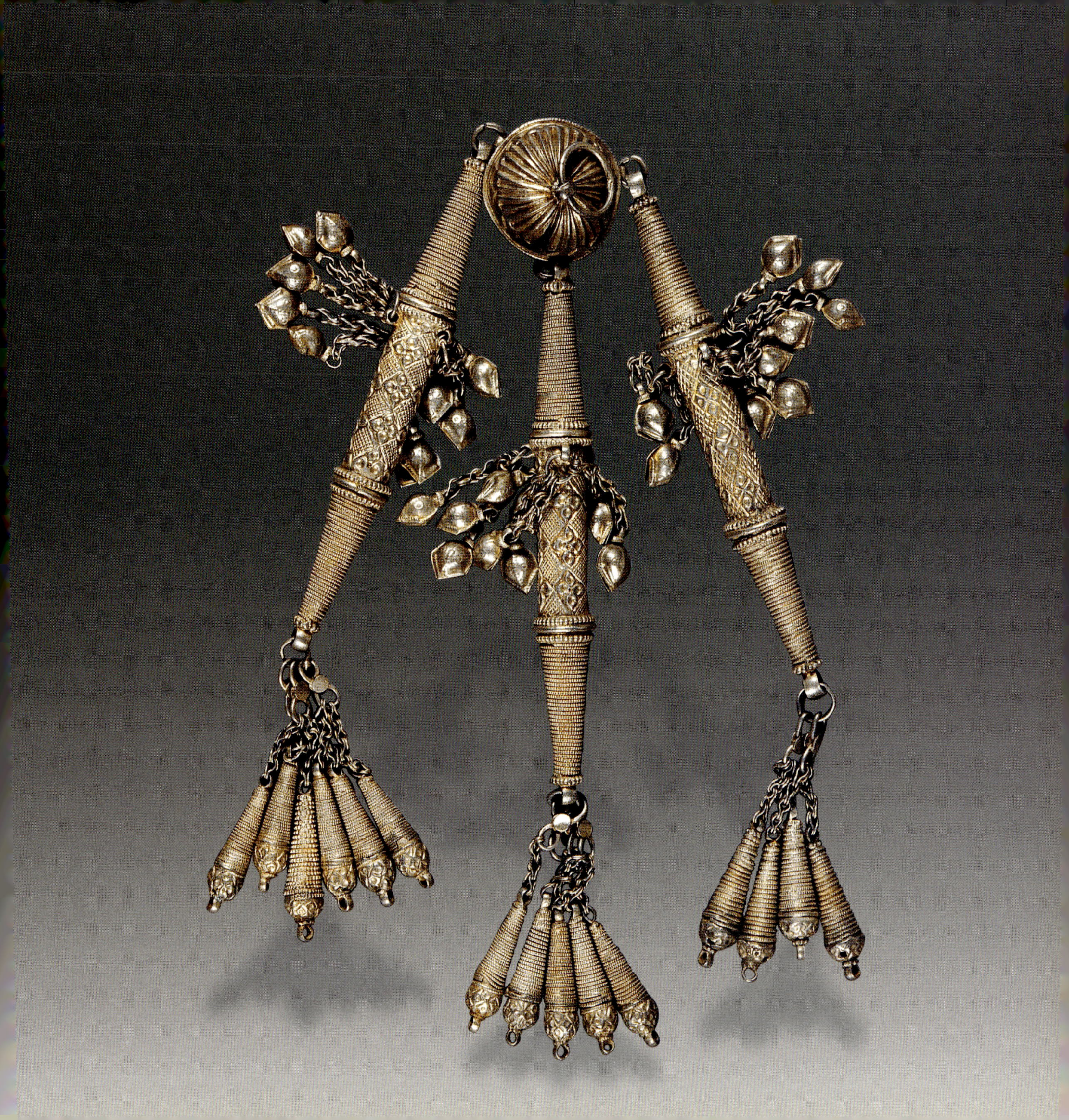

highlight hairstyles, with the same function but, of course, with different names in various parts of India. Silver pins may be clipped on either side of centrally parted long hair. Most pins are plain but some are decorated with small ornate pendants worked with enamelling or engraving. In ancient Indian literature, *garbha* was the term used for a pin, sometimes referred to as 'a chain to tie up the hair'.

In present-day Bengal, the pin is called *kanta nakshatra phul* or *pan kanta*. *Sisphul*, *chaunk* or *choti phul* are the terms used for a round boss worn on the hair just above the forehead. *Sir maang* is a chain and pendant worn on the head by Hindus, while *boda* is an ornament woven in silk and silver and plaited into the hair of children. In descriptions found in Sanskrit literature, the ornament used to embellish the braid is called *malya apir* and *balapaiya*. The North Indian word for a long braid is *chunti*; a silver ornament of the same name has three to five tiers of silver tassels and is conventionally tied to the lower end of the braid by newly married Hindu and Muslim women. In Himachal Pradesh, an ornament called *morpatti* (literally, peacock strap) is worn on the head like a *jhumka* (bunch) to adorn the hair.

HEAD AND FOREHEAD ORNAMENTS

The hair was bestowed with great attention in ancient India and women decorated their head and hair with feathers and flowers. Even today many women, especially in West and South India, adorn their hair with flowers, even using gold and silver to make floral patterns. A variety of braid and bun ornaments are made of silver to

Above:
Silver chukphool *(head ornament) with seven tiny pendants and attached bells hanging from a disc engraved with floral motifs, 20th century, North India*

Forehead adornments are also widely worn all over India, the designs varying from region to region. Circular, hemispherical or crescent-moon shaped pendants are tied with long chains and rest on the forehead, hanging from the hair parting, while the chain is attached to the braid or bun at the back of the head. In North India, the *tika* or *tilak* is worn. In Rajasthan it is known as *jhela* and in Gujarat as *damani*, while in Tamil Nadu, this ornament is known as *thalaikkachchu*. Some of these pieces comprise of three chains in which one is attached to a pendant and the other two are separated from the middle parting to terminate at the ear-lobes. An alternate style is *jhumar*, which is a triangular ornament and is worn on one side of the forehead. *Bindi* is a small tinsel forehead ornament, traditionally circular, but varying in shape according to the wearer's preference. Elaborate *bindis* are popular and are considered an integral part of an Indian woman's attire. In Kashmir, women wear an ornament similar to the *jhumar* on the front of the forehead; these are made of silver, with beautiful floral designs and small *ghungarus* (bells) on them. Although forehead ornaments are worn all over India, they are used more by the tribal women of Orissa, Madhya Pradesh and Rajasthan and among Muslim women of Uttar Pradesh, Bihar and Punjab.

NOSE AND EAR ORNAMENTS

Most scholars believe that the nose ornament is of Arabic origin and that it was not worn in India before the advent of the Muslims. Mediaeval visitors to India, such as Tavernier, have said in their travelogues that Arabian women wore hollow rings of gold or silver between their nostrils and silver rings around their eyes to protect them from the desert sun's rays. But this theory of the origin of nose ornaments from Arabia may not be

Below:
Silver pair of balas *(earrings) in spiral designs and small chains dangling from the hoops, 20th century, North India*

Below:
Part of a heavy silver kangan *(bangle) with stylized grooves, 20th century, North India*

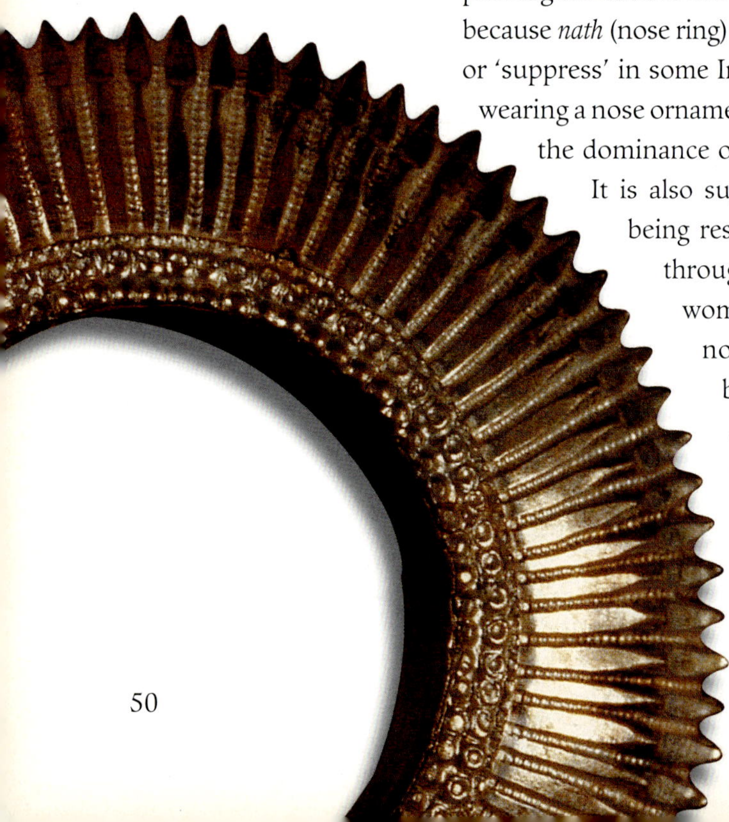

accurate. Hindu manuscripts, such as Bilhan's *Rasamanjari*, dated AD1080, refers to the nose ring (*nasavansavinimukta mukta falam*) as do treatises such as *Lakihman Desika* (eleventh century AD), *Lila Charita* (AD1250) and *Vallabh Deva* (fifteenth century AD). A mural painting (fourteenth century AD) at the Tiruvambadi shrine at Thiruvananthapuram shows women wearing nose rings studded with pearls.

Called *nath*, *nathia* or *bulaki* in North India and *mukkuthtai* or *bulaki* in South India, nose ornaments are popular among both Hindu and Muslim women of India. These are usually worn in pierced nostrils, but nose clips are now also becoming popular. Some women are opposed to piercing the nostrils and wearing nose rings because *nath* (nose ring) means 'to control' or 'suppress' in some Indian dialects and wearing a nose ornament would connote the dominance of women by men. It is also suggestive of a bull being restrained by a rope through its nose. Some women, however, wear nose rings in the belief that it is auspicious. There is quite a variety of styles in nose rings worn in India. Some of these are:

Nath: a large nose ring studded with precious gems.

Bulak: a pendant hung on either side of the nose or strung on a *nath*.

Latkan: a pendant slung on a thin silver ring (*nath*).

Laung or *keel*: a small stud, with a pearl or turquoise in it, in the shape of a *laung* (clove) worn in the flesh of one nostril (sometimes both nostrils are pierced).

Phulee: a small ring with a single oval-shaped stone as a pendant.

Nathini: a small ring worn on the left nostril by young girls.

Ear ornaments are almost mandatory accessories for a Hindu woman and wearing them is considered both becoming and auspicious. Earrings also have specific significance, denoting a married woman. According to the philosopher Shankara, in his treatise *Saundarya Lahiri*, Lord Shiva's immortality is attributed to the power of his mother's *tantakar* (ear ornaments). The verse of *Saundarya Lahiri* that mentions Shiva has been interpreted by mediaeval commentators to mean that the sun and the moon are *tantakars* adorning Devi's (Shiva's consort, goddess Parvati) ears and are hence under her aegis. The commencement, duration and the end of time are directed by the sun and the moon and so are virtually controlled by the *tantakar* worn by Devi. As the earring is attributed with much significance, it is customary for young girls to have their ears pierced before they are a year old. The ear-piercing ceremony called *kanachedan sanskar*, is traditionally performed on an auspicious day and is one of the important *sanskaran* (ceremonies) of Hindu families. In some parts of India, the ears of boys are also pierced and they wear silver or gold earrings, commensurate with their means.

Ear ornaments were an important feature in Indian decorative arts. Several artefacts of ear ornaments from the Indus Valley civilization and the Maurya, Sunga, Satavahana, Kushana and Gupta periods as well as the mediaeval period have been excavated. Certain designs of ear ornament – annular, reel and amphora – worn in the Harappan, Mauryan and Kushana periods are in existence in remote parts of India even today.

The remains of a man's skeleton from the Neolithic period (c. 6000 BC) found in the pre-Harappan town of Mehargarh included square mother-of-pearl earrings in his ears. The reason why he wore earrings might have been esoteric protection or tribal and personal identification, or could have been for aesthetic or medical reasons. Ear-piercing has been used in traditional cures – in acupuncture,for instance, the point of incision is at the centre of the ear-lobe. The specific spot that is pierced in the ear is also determined by social or religious customs of a community.

In Kashmir and Punjab, ear ornaments are called *bala, lakha kundas, bali, karnaphool, jhumka, kantala, laung* and *khaleel*. In Uttar Pradesh and its adjoining areas, the names are similar to Delhi where designs from the Mughal period are popular. In South India, they are called *karnapoo vooloo* and *zalli gileeloo*. In Kashmir, Muslim women wear earrings called *kona vaji*, supported by decorative pink chains passing over the

Above:
Silver armlet capped by a conical silver piece and covered with exquisite patterns; it is clasped by a slip and press system, 20th century, North India

Above:
Double-stringed silver locket, with the figure of Lord Ganesh in the oval-shaped centre, encircled with leaf patterns in high relief; the locket is worn as a religious talisman, 20th century, Central India

crown of the head and attached to the hair. In Himachal Pradesh, silver earrings (*bala*) with pendants attached to chains hooked to the hair for support, are popular. In Orissa, most earrings, called *karanphool*, cover the entire ear and are embellished with filigree work. The earrings are supported by chains, that pass over the top of the ears and are hooked to the hair. The spiralled cobra is a popular design for this type of earring. Some traditional types of ear ornaments are:

Bali: a set of rings worn round the edge of the ear.
Karanphool/jhumka: a flower-shaped stud with a bell or bud-shaped drop suspended from it.
Bala or *kungridar*: a heavy, fringed earring.

Ear ornaments are often described in exchanges between lovers. In a song from a Hindi film a girl asks her friend to search for one of her missing earrings – she is worried that her secret meeting with her lover may be discovered because of her negligence. In a Gujarati folk song, Radha teases Krishna about how his ear ornaments were replaced by feminine earrings. Similar references in popular culture reflect the prominence of earrings in the Hindu scheme of things.

NECK ORNAMENTS

By most standards of beauty, a woman is considered beautiful if she has a long neck. Garlands of flowers were used centuries ago to decorate the neck (and still are), so flower garlands can be considered the predecessor of the necklace in India.

Different kinds of necklaces were worn by women and men and the names of these necklaces vary, depending on the designs. *Hansuli*, choker, necklace, chain, *thali, champakali* and *vayjantimala* are some ornaments worn on the neck.

A *hansuli* is a circular neck ornament that rests on the collar-bone – it is worn mostly by Rajasthani women. A choker is a flexible necklace worn around the neck. A chain is a long necklace without a pendant; it is called a necklace if it has a pendant. A *thali* is a *mangalsutra* (necklace of a married woman) worn by the women of South India, while a *champakali* is a necklace made of beads in the shape of *champa* (*Michelia champaca*) buds. A *vayjantimala* is a necklace, rather like a garland, referred to in the *Puranas*; this type of garland is said to have been worn by Lord Vishnu.

In ancient Indian literature, the following terms were used for different types of neck ornaments:

Pralambika: a long necklace hanging down to the navel.
Haar: necklace of beads.
Hansuli: a ring or collar, thick in the middle and tapering at both ends.

The women of Himachal Pradesh wear long silver necklaces made of silver bud-shaped pendants or diamond-shaped silver medallions, set with semi-precious stones. The chains are made in different designs: simple, small, interconnected rings or tiny rosettes held together with silver bands, worked beautifully with blue or green enamel. In South India, women wear necklaces made of gold or silver coins.

HAND ORNAMENTS

Bracelets, *pahunchian, churi, kangan, kara, bajuband, bazuband,* bangles and armlets are the various types of hand ornaments. Bangles were worn as early as the Harappan period, the most fascinating example being the bangles worn by a bronze dancing girl from the Harappan period, with her shapely wrists and hands covered with ornaments. Excavations

Below:
Wide bangle made of silver in the cutwork technique, skirted with small bells

Facing Page: Ornate silver belt in a silver thread net design, the top portion embellished with round coins and butterfly shapes, 20th century, North India

Right: Close-up of the silver belt's centre, decorated with circular and rectangular designs in high relief

have uncovered bangles made of shell, terracotta and bronze from almost all the sites of the Indus Valley civilization, and of gold and silver from some sites. These findings indicate the popularity of this ornament among people in the Harappan region. Bangles have continued to be one of the most favoured pieces of jewellery and have been depicted in several sculptures and paintings all through Indian history. Even today, glass bangles are part of daily wear in North India, while gold and silver ones are worn on special occasions. Women in South India generally prefer gold bangles. The variety of shapes, sizes and designing styles of hand ornaments reflects the popularity of this adornment. They include:

Bajuband: a trinket adorned with semi-circular silver or gold pieces that are hollowed out and filled with melted resin. The ends are furnished with loops of silver, and secured by silken skeins.

Kara: a ring worn on the wrist.

Padak: amulets of various shapes

Pahunchian: a broad bracelet that is shaped in small pointed prisms of solid silver or hollows of gold filled with melted resin.

Hathphool: an ornament for the back of the *hath* (hand). The rich spherical plate in the centre is attached to chains made of clove-shaped drops with links in shapely forms attached to two rings for the first and fourth fingers and to a bracelet from the wrist.

Kangan: a ring with ornamented ends in animal-head shapes. Tiger, elephant and dragon heads are the most popular.

Armlet: a bracelet worn on the upper arm

WAIST-BAND

Kamarpatta or *kamarpatti* is a waist-band, that was used in ancient India by both

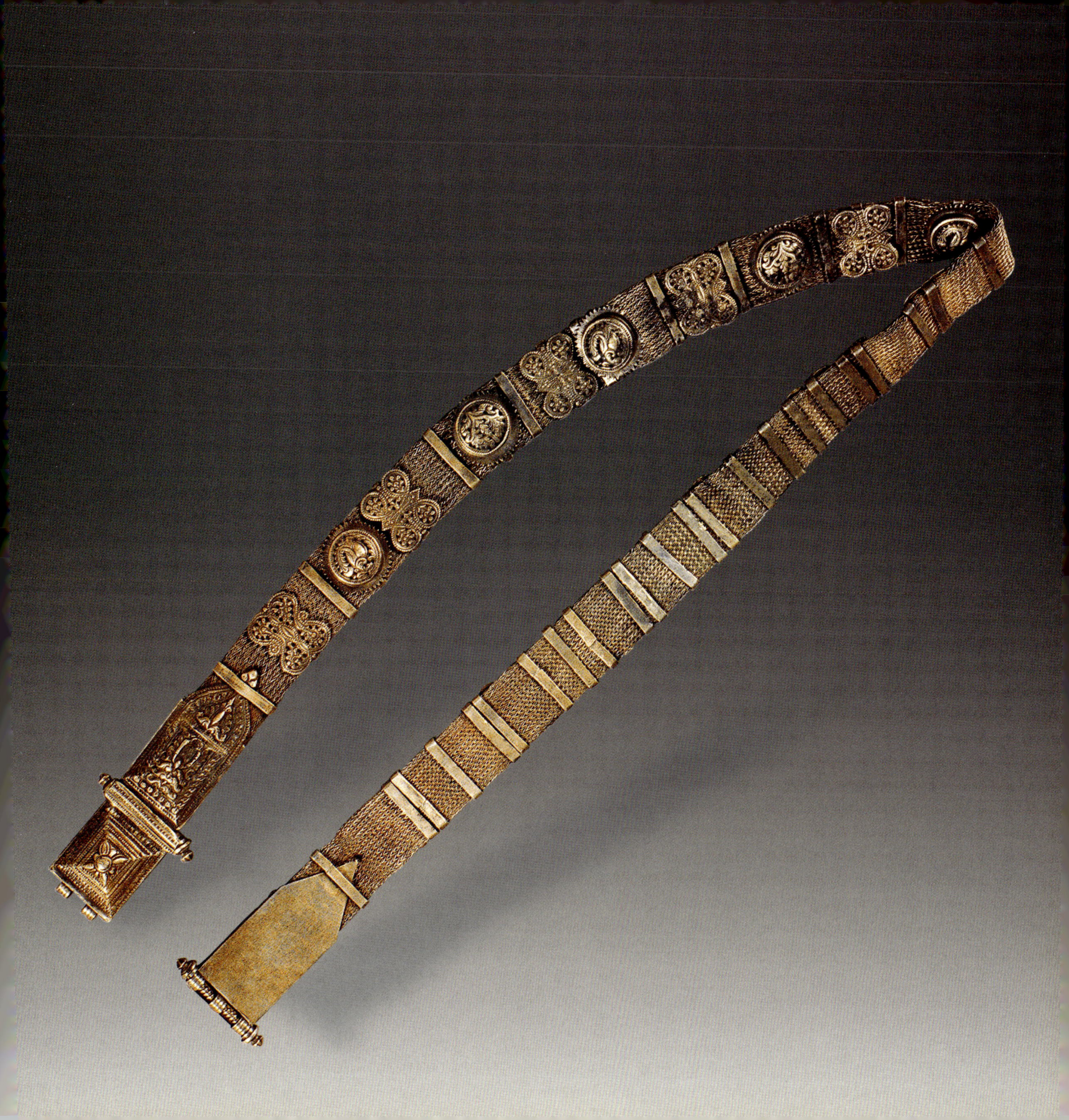

Above:
Close-ups of the buckles at both ends of the silver belt on the facing page

Right:
Silver anklet in four parts, each interlocked with spring lockets, 20th century, North India; the reverse of the anklet is shown on the facing page

men and women, clasped over the lower garment. Stone, terracotta and bronze sculptures throughout Indian history, especially the images of *yaksha*s and *yakshi*s (nature deities) of the second-first century BC testify to their use. Later, during the Mughal period, it was worn over the *choga* or *angarkha* (upper garment) by royals, courtesans and noblemen and were made of gold, silver, precious stones, and sometimes even fabric, commensurate with the status of the wearer. Royalty and the elite wore *kamarpattis* studded with precious stones, otherwise *kamarpattis* made of silver were generally worn. Waist-bands made of precious metals were generally plain or of the simple flat-ring variety, encircling the waist and ending with beautifully designed clasps and intricately carved with floral patterns or animal heads. In some North Indian communities, it is a customary ornament for weddings.

ANKLETS

Anklets were probably worn from the very beginning of Indian history. Literary texts like the Ramayana, Mahabharata, the *Puranas*, Kalidas's epics and Sangam literature refer in detail to the types of jewellery used by both men and women. Stone, terracotta and bronze sculptures from the Sunga period (second–first century BC) to the Nayak period (sixteenth–seventeenth century), illustrate

women with anklets. From the visual depictions it appears that anklets were initially circular. Later, these rings became broader and acquired different names, depending on the place and language.

These ornaments called *kanachedan sanskar* were made of silver and worn by the common man. *Paizeb* is a Persian term for anklet; they are usually made with chains and pendants of silver, which clink together when the wearer walks. Similar to a chain, it is comprised of heavy rings of silver, rather like a *hansuli* or neck ornament. In some communities, anklets were ring-shaped, very substantial and heavy. Rajasthani women wear engraved silver anklets known as *neoroi*.

Khungru is a ring or anklet of long ornamental silver beads and *tora* is a heavy ornament made of a set of chains with a broad clasp.

TOE-RING

Anwat is a Hindi term used for a ring with little bells, worn on the big toe. *Bichhua* or *chhalle* is a ring worn on the big toe. In Central India, these toe-rings are sometimes linked together to form a set similar to the *hathphool* for the hands – the toe-rings are linked by bands of bars. In most parts of the country, it is customary for married women to wear silver toe-rings. The rings are usually flat but sometimes the upper part has floral patterns, fish designs or geometric patterns on them.

Forehead pendants *(maang-tika)* to anklets, ornaments are valued possessions for all women. With the aesthetic taste of Indian women and their inherent love for jewellery, the ancient heritage and tradition of jewellery has been well preserved. Today, silver jewellery retains its ethnic charm, blended with contemporary designs.

Above:
Reverse side of silver anklet shown on p.56, ornamented with dotted designs in the relief technique, 20th century, North India

INDIAN SILVER COINAGE

Coins, often discovered during archaeological excavations or accidentally during digging operations, play a vital role in the study of history. They illuminate and reconstruct historical events that cannot be gleaned from other sources, and substantiate and confirm the historical data derived from these sources. We do not have sufficient ancient Indian literature that could have served as historical evidence if classical writers had recorded events of the period they lived in. However, facts about rulers, their names, dynasties, hobbies and interests, religions and the economic condition of the time come to light in many instances from coins. For example, we know exclusively from coins that nearly thirty Bactrian kings and queens ruled over the Punjab for about a hundred years during 200–100 BC. This remarkable historical era was revealed after nearly 2,000 years only through the discovery of their coins in gold, silver and copper. Similarly, although there is a reference to the Satavahana rulers of the Deccan in the *Puranas* and in epigraphical records, the dates and events of their rule were corroborated only after the finding of Satavahana coins in the latter half of the twentieth century. Another instance is of Mughal emperor Akbar, who is known to have been a secular king, and mentioned as such in many references to the Mughal period. However, this fact was substantiated only when his coins, with portraits of Hindu divinities, Rama and Sita, engraved on them, were found. Coins, thus, play an important role in making an authentic mosaic of society, culture, religion, art, music and the aesthetic values of a state or country.

Gold, it is believed, was used in India as currency. The use of the word *hiranya*

Facing Page:
Silver bent bar coin with geometrical designs (the sun) on the obverse side; the reverse side is plain, 6th century BC

Right (top and centre): *Silver Janapada coin with engravings of various symbols on the obverse (top) and reverse (centre) sides, 5th century* BC, *Andhra Janapada*

Right (bottom): *Silver coin in an irregular shape, with engravings of symbols, 5th–4th century* BC, *North India, Magadha empire*

(literally gold) in Vedic literature led to this inference. But in this context, *hiranya* meant metal in general, and may have been *rajat* (white) or *pita* or *suvarna* (yellow). Only later, the adjective *rajat*, without the noun *hiranya*, came to denote silver. In the Vedic period, however, *hiranya* was used in its original sense (metal) and it implied only metal used as currency. This was so even as late as the Gupta period. Only silver was used in transactions as is evident both from the hoard of silver coins and metallic pieces found with them.

Coins had not begun to be minted in India during the Vedic period. In *Ashtadhyayi*, a work of grammar by Panini dated the sixth–fifth century BC, there is a *sutra* (verse), which shows that metallic pieces were stamped (*ahata*) with symbols (*rupa*). *Ashtadhyayi* also refers to coins as *karshapana* and *sona*. This, however, implies that by this time the use of coins had reached an advanced stage and it may be assumed that considerable time would have elapsed between this period and the first minting of coins, that coins in their final form had originated long before the time of Panini's *Ashtadhyayi*. It may also be assumed, on the basis of historical conclusions and supported by nuismatic evidence, that coins took their form not long after in the seventh century BC. It may be claimed that coins had originated in India at least a century before Lydia and China had even thought of them.

The earliest Indian coins known so far, dated to about the sixth century BC, are made of silver and are called punch-mark coins. These coins were punched with different symbols, often sun, tree, animal and hill symbols and geometric designs. They had no written inscriptions, but the number of symbols ran into several hundreds. A symbol or a group of symbols were confined to the coins of a particular area or to a specific variety or type. This helps to distinguish the coins of one area or state from that of the other and of one period from another. The technique of punching coins is unique to India

Historical accounts have not recorded how coins were manufactured in ancient India. A passage in Kautilya's *Arthashastra* lists some objects that were used in the minting of coins. Metal was first melted in crucibles and purified with alkalis. It was then beaten into sheets on an anvil with a hammer, cut into pieces with clippers, and finally stamped with dies or punches, with symbols etched on them. Except for the use of automatic devices, almost the same process is used even today in the minting of coins all over the world.

Punch-mark silver coins are of two types: imperial and local. The actual coins of the period show that they were cut and clipped to adjust them for weight. Unlike today's coins, these were made in every conceivable shape – round, oval or elliptical. Sometimes, the metal for the desired weight of the coin was melted and poured onto the ground or onto a flat board, and left to take its own shape. Pellets were also sometimes made from molten metal, and then flattened. The flam or planchet thus prepared was impressed on one side by means of punching bearing devices. (The idea was probably taken from the practice of branding cattle used in transactions or reared as part of a household's wealth during the Vedic period. The number of the symbols later increased to two and then gradually to five.)

Silver punch-mark coins stopped being issued some time in the second century BC, but coinage continued to exert a wide influence over the next 400 to 500 years.

Along with pieces of golden jewellery, some silver metallic pieces of a uniform size and weight have also been found in Mohenjodaro. According to some scholars, these silver pieces may have been used as coins. The earliest reference to silver coins was found from Mesopotamia. This written evidence in cuneiform script is about 4,500 years old and referred to a payment that was made in silver metallic pieces – these may have been silver coins.

Until the Mauryan period, coins of only one denomination, weighing 52 grains, were known throughout the empire. They were identified as *pana*, and also known as *karshapana*. According to the *Arthashastra*, silver coins of four denominations – *pana*, *ardhapana* (half *pana*), *pada* (quarter *pana*) and *ashtabhaga*

Left (top and centre): *Oval coin in silver, with floral patterns on the obverse side and a plain reverse side, 5th century, Kashi Janapada, Uttar Pradesh*

or *ardhapadika* (one-eighth *pana*) were subsequently issued from the mint of the Mauryan empire.

Two very important silver coins were issued by Alexander the Great of Greece, who invaded India in the third century BC, after he returned from the border of India. These silver coins were minted by Alexander in Babylonia and depicted the scene of war between Porus, Indian ruler of Paurava, and Alexander. The silver coins are called decadrachms and tetradrachms. The figure on the coins is identified as Alexander in the form of the Greek god Zeus and he is being crowned by Nike, the goddess of victory. On the reverse side, is a charging horseman with a lance and a retreating elephant, with two men on its back turning to face their pursuer. Perhaps these Indo-Greek coins comprised the first system of coinage to be associated with India. These coins were usually bilingual, with Greek inscriptions on the obverse and the local Kharoshti script on the reverse.

Important changes made by Alexander in the minting of coins had a lasting impression on later coins. The tradition of his silver coins, which featured the figure of Heracles on the obverse side and the Greek god Zeus on the reverse side, was followed by the Indo-Greek, Indo-Bactrian, Saka, Kushana and even Gupta rulers. Other foreign rulers who invaded India and ruled for some time also issued silver coins with these features. Demetrius (200–190 BC) Agathacles (190–180 BC) and Partaleon (190–185 BC) issued their coins with Greek, Brahmi and Kharoshti inscriptions or with Indian gods, such as Krishna and Balrama on them. After the

Facing Page: (top) *Silver coin (tetradrachm) struck by Alexander the Great, 3rd century BC* ***(centre)*** *Indo-Scythian silver coin, with a city goddess holding a palm frond and lamp on the reverse and the image of a king on horseback, encircled by the Bactrian script on the obverse, 1st century BC* ***(bottom left)*** *Reverse of round Indo-Greek silver coin (drachm), with the profile of King Hermeous (the last Indo-Greek ruler) on the obverse and an enthroned Zeus encircled by a Kharoshti inscription on the reverse, 1st century BC*

Left:
Struck by Appolodotus I is this square silver Indo-Greek coin (drachm), with and an elephant engraved on the obverse side and a bull on the reverse, 3rd century BC

Below: (left and centre) *Struck by Buddhagupta of the Gupta dynasty is this silver coin, displaying the profile of the king on the obverse and a fan-tailed* garuda *(eagle) surrounded by the Brahmi script on the reverse, 5th–6th century* BC

Mauryan rulers, local rulers minted some coins in their own names but most of these were in gold or copper; only a few silver coins were found of local rulers of tribal republics, such as the Vemakis, Audumberas, Kunindas and Youdheyas. Silver coins of the Youdheyas depict a standing Kartikeya (supreme commander of the divine army) figure with six heads and a spear in his hand along with an -

Towards the beginning of the fourth century AD, the dynasty of the Gupta emperors rose out of a small principality in what is now eastern Uttar Pradesh and Bihar. They established their empire comprising all of North India and ruled for 200 years. The first king of this dynasty was Chandragupta I who ruled from 319 to 350 AD. Samudragupta, Chandragupta II, Vikramaditya, Kumaragupta, and

inscription in the Brahmi script. On the reverse side, a six-headed goddess stands on a lotus with hill symbols, Nandi (bull) and a tree. Even in the Kushana period (second century BC), coins were issued in the Indo-Greek style although most of the coins were minted in gold and bronze. A silver coin depicting the face of King Kujul Kadphises and a horse-rider on the obverse side, with a Greek inscription on the reverse side, has also been found.

Skandagupta succeeded him and ruled during the period known as the golden or classical period of ancient Indian history, a high point in Indian civilization.

The later Gupta kings issued their coins in gold, silver, bronze and other metals. Initially, they copied the style of Kushana coins but they later refined their minting quality and the depiction of figures and details. Silver coins were not known to the early Gupta rulers.

They were first introduced during Chandragupta II's time, in 409 AD, when he came into contact with the Malwa region states, in what is presently Raipur, Bilaspur, Indore and Ujjain in Central India. These silver coins are very similar to the western Kshatrapa coins. The king's bust appears on the obverse side with the date (during the Gupta era). On the reverse side is a figure of a *garuda* (falcon).

coins were minted in gold during the period and that silver coins were very few in comparison. This was because the Gupta period was a very rich period in Indian history.

Several rulers of the Deccan area also minted silver coins. The earliest among them were the rulers of the Satavahana dynasty who ruled during the first and second centuries AD, probably in what is

Left: *Issued by King Visvasena, this silver coin is embellished with the name of the king in the Brahmi script on the reverse, 3rd century AD*

Kumaragupta I also followed his father by issuing silver coins for the Gujarat and Saurashtra states. He started two new types of coins by replacing the *garuda* figure with that of a peacock for eastern India. During the reigns of Skandagupta and Buddhagupta, some silver coins were also continued for the benefit of the states. On the basis of the hoards of Gupta coinage recovered, we can say that most

now Andhra Pradesh, but they minted very few silver coins. Vashishti Putra Pulumavi minted a silver coin based on coins of the Kshatrapa ruler Nahapana. On its obverse side, is a figure of a king with his name inscribed in the Brahmi script. On the reverse, symbols of the sun god and a hillock are etched, with an inscription in the South Indian Brahmi or another Dravidian script.

Above:
Silver coin issued in the name of Mughal emperor Shah Alam II by Maratha ruler Shivaji Rao Holkar of Malwa, 1886–1903: the central image of the sun is encircled with a Nagari inscription on the obverse (right) while a Persian inscription is on the reverse (centre)

Above:
Silver coin of Gurjar Pratihara king Bhoj Dev I, with the figure of a varaha *(boar) on the obverse and the Devanagari script on the reverse, 10th century* AD

Contemporary to the Satavahana dynasty were the western Saka Kshatrapa kings, who ruled in North India. These rulers also minted the famous silver coins based on the model of the Indo-Greek silver coins. On the obverse side of these silver coins is a figure of the king and an inscription in Greek, and on the reverse side is an image of a thunderbolt and arrows with an inscription in the Brahmi and Kharosthi scripts. After the Hun king Gautami Putra Satkarni defeated the Satavahanas, silver coins of the Kshatrapa ruler Nahapana were re-struck on both sides with the name of the Satavahana king. A treasure trove of such coins was found in the village Jogal Thambi in Nasik district (Maharashtra).

After the fall of the Gupta dynasty, the Huns established their seat in North India. The more prominent kings were Tormana and Mihirkula who ruled from 520–528 AD. Both kings issued silver coins with their profiles on the obverse side and fire altars with two attendants on the reverse. These coins also have some inscriptions engraved on them.

Another major dynasty that ruled after the fall of the Guptas was that of Vardhana of Thaneshwar who ruled during the sixth–seventh century AD: a famous king of this dynasty was Harshavardhana. There are very few coins from this period, but among those found is a famous silver coin in which the bust of the king is in profile on the obverse side and a peacock with an inscription around it is on the reverse. During the ninth–tenth century AD, the Gurjar Pratihara dynasty of North India also minted some silver coins. These coins, smaller and thicker and with a silver base, were called *gadhaiya paisa* or *drammas* in the mid-ninth century AD. Criss-crossing the region of Kabul and Gandhara were the great trade routes

Below:
Punch-marked Pandyan coin bearing symbols on the obverse and the royal fish emblem on the reverse, 3rd–2nd century BC*, South India*

from Central Asia, Khorasan and North India. The Hindu Shahis who ruled these areas exploited the rich silver deposits of the Panjhir Valley and minted silver coins depicting horsemen and bulls in action, considerably influencing Indian currencies for a couple of centuries more.

The Cholas, Cheras, Chalukyas and Pandyas ruled South India for several centuries. The history of coinage in Tamil Nadu dates from the pre-Christian era and presents a picture of an almost continuous minting of currencies, down to the seventeenth century AD, with a brief break from the fifth–seventh centuries AD. Sangam literature (first–third century AD) also contains several references to coins of different kinds. Among them are references to silver punch-mark and die-struck coins. Several hoards of silver punch-mark coins have been found all over Tamil Nadu and Kerala and these coins are attributed to the merchant guilds of both the North and South. Silver punch-mark coins of the Chera period have been found in large numbers in Madurai and Tirunelveli, each with five symbols on the obverse side and a stylized fish on the reverse.

The Cholas also issued regular coinage in silver though they were fewer than the gold and copper coins. Rajendra Chola I (AD1012–1044) struck silver coins with the name of Uttam Chola engraved on them, while Rajaraja I also issued silver coins with the symbols of a tiger, a bow, a fish, and a Nagari inscription on them.

Thirty-one silver coins were discovered among a valuable treasure found at Vaigaikulam in Tirunelveli district of Kerala. These coins were from the reign of the Chera rulers who ruled in south and central Kerala in the eleventh–twelfth century AD. The silver coins were die-struck with a scene from a Nagari legend, with an open-mouthed crocodile figure engraved on them.

Below:
The Persian script is boldly engraved on both sides of this silver coin, proclaiming the name of Bahmani king Tajuddin Firuz Shah II (AD 1397–1422) and the date of the coin's issue

After the Chera period, the Chalukyas of Kalyani issued both silver and gold coins during the tenth–twelfth centuries AD. The silver coins were inscribed with legends in Kannada and symbols of the lotus and *varaha* (boar). The Yadavas of Devgiri who ruled from the

twelfth–fourteenth centuries AD in the north Deccan area also minted silver coins, which were in continuous use and played an important role in the economic history of the Deccan.

The mediaeval coinage of India includes those of the Arabs, the Turks and the Mughals and covers a period of over eleven centuries beginning from the eighth–ninth centuries AD when the earliest silver coins of this period were minted by the governor of Sind. A hoard of these silver coins have been found in the Marwar-Jodhpur region. Their discovery indicates continuous trade contacts between the Arab Caliphate in the Middle East and peninsular India in the ninth to thirteenth centuries AD. Mahmud Ghazni (AD 1001–1030) who invaded India and annexed the Punjab, issued silver coins (*tankas* or *dirhams*) for Indian territories. These are the earliest Islamic coins of silver in India that show the influence of the indigenous tradition. These coins bear the *kalima* in the Arabic script on the obverse side and an exact rendering in Sanskrit on the reverse. It is believed that Al-Biruni, the scholar, mathematician and astronomer, who was in the sultan's entourage when he came to India, may have helped in composing the Sanskrit inscription for these *tankas*.

The Sultanate of Delhi issued several coins in various metals like gold, silver and copper; the silver *tankas* were abundant. Silver might have come from Central Asia during this period. In addition, an alloy of silver and copper was also used to issue coins by the early sultans. The weight equation between

Below: (left)
Silver coin of Muhammad Shah Durrani of Kashmir with the name of the king and the dates of his rule inscribed in Persian on both sides

Facing Page: (top)
Silver tankha *(coin) of Alauddin Khilji, sultan of Delhi (1296–1316), with the title 'Victorious King' inscribed on both sides in Persian;* **(centre)** *Silver rupee issued by Islam Shah Suri (1545–1552), with an inscription in the Devanagari script on the reverse;* **(below)** *Struck by Ghiyasuddin Tughlaq, ruler of North India (1320–1325), this silver* tankha *has his name inscribed on both sides*

Below: (left and centre) *Mughal emperor Babur (1515–1530) struck this silver* shahrukhi *(coin) with the* kalima *and the names of the four Caliphs on the obverse side and the emperor's name and titles on the reverse;* ***(right)*** *Obverse side of silver coin issued by Mughal emperor Humayun (1530–1556), bearing kalima and the four Caliph*s

gold and silver coins was kept as uniform as possible. Pure silver coinage was scarce in North India, but it was more abundant in Bengal where silver may have come from a more easterly source of supply. The Bengal silver was used by the Turkish sultans for coining money when Bengal came under their control.

The earliest silver *tankas* of the sultans who ruled India portrayed a galloping horseman surrounded by a small inscription on the margin on the obverse while the reverse side is engraved with an Arabic inscription. In Indian monetary history, these coins have great significance. Iltutmish (AD 1210–1235) issued a further series of silver coins (*tankas*), weighing 175 grains each. Iltutmish is credited with the standardization of Delhi's coinage; his currency reform was noteworthy and was adopted by the successive sultans of Delhi. Razia Sultan, queen of the Slave dynasty who ruled only for three years (AD 1236–1239), minted silver coins in the name of her father, Iltutmish. The silver *tanka,* with an inscription of the Caliph of Baghdad was adopted by the rulers of the Slave dynasty.

The Khilji dynasty of the Delhi Sultanate also minted coins in silver. Several silver coins with high silver content from Alauddin Khilji's reign have been discovered. The square silver coins he issued surpassed even those of Muhammad bin Tughlaq in their execution and form. But the coinage of Muhammad bin Tughlaq (AD 1325–1351) was of a higher standard of technical execution and was far superior to those of the Khiljis. He initially issued traditional silver coins but later, on an experimental basis, introduced a new silver coin of nine grains called the Adali, but it failed due to mismanagement.

Sher Shah Suri's (AD 1540–1545) reforms in the coinage system of India are noteworthy. He continued to circulate the silver coins of Iltutmish, but with an altered weight system. His silver coins were of a broad flan, that is, the rupee became the standard coin with a lower denomination. Inscriptions on the coins follow the traditional pattern with the *kalima* and the citation of the first four Caliphs on one side, and the names of the sultans, dates and mint on the reverse. Sher Shah Suri changed the original design and adopted the king's name in Nagari characters instead. The name of the mints where the coins were struck were often inscribed in the margin of the coins. Sher Shah Suri established several mints at many places and these were subsequently used by his successors.

MUGHAL SILVER COINAGE (AD 1526–1857)

When Babur, a descendant of the Mongol Timur, invaded the Lodi territories and defeated the Lodi king Ibrahim Lodi in the battle of Panipat in AD 1526, he stayed on to establish the Mughal empire in India. Babur, however, did not consolidate his empire and after his death, his son Humayun ascended the throne to inherit a troubled kingdom.

Below: (left) *Reverse side of Humayun's coin (facing page, right), bearing his name and titles;* ***(centre and right)*** *Square silver rupee coin issued by Mughal emperor Jahangir (1605–1628)*

Below:
Square silver Mughal coin (obverse and reverse) of Jahangir, issued from Lahore

Humayun was briefly overthrown by Sher Shah Suri but he managed to regain control of his kingdom in 1555. The coins of these two founders of the Mughal rule in India were the pure Central Asian type – thin silver dirhams, similar to Timurind coinage. After Humayun's death, his son Jalaluddin Muhammad Akbar ascended

Facing Page:
Top: (left and right) *Silver coin struck by Shahjahan (1628–1658);*
(centre) *Zodiac rupee coin struck by Jahangir, with the Aries sign on the obverse and the emperor's name and date of minting on the reverse;*
(bottom) *Commemorating Din-i-Ilahi, propagated by Akbar (1556–1605), is this rare silver coin, Lahore, 16th century*

the throne. It was during this period (AD 1556–1605) that the finest currencies (an example is the coin issued in honour of Dil-i-Ilahi, Akbar's new secular religion) were produced and they continued for over three centuries until 1857 when the Mughal empire was overthrown by the British.

The Mughal coinage was a combination of mediaeval Islamic and Hindu influences. The Mughals inherited the system of minting coinage from the Sultanate period and from Sher Shah Suri. The Mughal rulers also minted rupees in silver from different mints in various denominations. The basic coin was the silver rupee and continued to be minted until 1950. Called the *rupaya*, it is still in use. The weight of these coins was 178 grains each and their alloy was never allowed to rise above four per cent. Jahangir and Aurangzeb increased the basic unit for commerce transactions and tax payments. The Mughal emperor who issued the most beautiful coins was Jahangir. Among the most remarkable examples of nuismatic art are his zodiacal coins representing each zodiac sign. The engravers of the Mughal period used calligraphy, abstract decoration and the adaptable Persian *nastaliq* script, to combine it with geometrical and floral arabesque and to inscribe coins with verses from the Koran, the names of the four Caliphs, the name of the ruler, his title, year of ascension to the throne, and the names of the mints. It was only during a short period of Akbar's reign that the *kalima* and Hijra dates were substituted by other inscriptions and by the Din-i-Ilahi date.

During Akbar's time, silver rupees were minted in fourteen mints of India while during Aurangzeb's time they were produced in forty mints. In spite of the diversity of the mints, the uniformity in the form and fabric of the mintage was

Below: ***(left and centre)***
Silver rupee coin was issued by Mughal emperor Aurangzeb (1658–1707); the obverse side bears the name of the emperor and the reverse side proclaims the date and place of minting
(right)
Machine-made silver rupee of Mughal emperor Shah Alam II minted at Surat

maintained. Silver rupees continued to be struck by the Mughal emperors after Aurangzeb until the last emperor, Bahadur Shah Zafar (AD 1837–1857). After this emperor's reign, the centre of authority weakened due to infighting in the family. Several small states became independent and European companies started minting coins in the name of the Mughal emperors.

The British overthrew the Mughals and captured the throne in 1857. The Mughal economy and rule was shattered, but the silver rupees which were created during the Mughal period, continued upto the modern period, ranking among the finest coinage in the world. During the eighteenth century, the Dutch, French and British participated in foreign trade with India, but after some time, the Dutch and French were completely edged out and the British monopolized Indian trade. They slowly established British supremacy in India, helped by the infighting of the Mughals, Marathas and other provincial states.

The British also struck coins in gold, silver and copper for their factory settlements, and later for the British-Indian territories from the Indian mints at Bombay, Madras and Calcutta. Initially, the British used the silver rupees which were minted during the Mughal period but from 1872 they struck European silver coinage called Anglina. In 1677, new rupees were issued with the inscription 'Rupees of Bombay' on them. From 1717 until 1778, the Bombay silver rupee

remained a standard British coin. In 1793, the Surat silver rupee of the Mughals was adopted as the main currency of the Bombay presidency.

The Madras mint issued silver coins of the well-known Arcot rupees. These coins were issued in the name of the Mughal emperor until machine-made coins replaced them in 1815. In addition to the Arcot rupees, the Madras mint also issued *fanams* and half *fanam*s in the name of the company. These depicted Vishnu on one side and two Cs, probably referring to the British monarch Charles II, on the other side. Of all the silver-series coins, the coin showing Vishnu on one side and a *gopuram* (temple tower) on the other side, are the best-executed coins of the Madras mint. The Company issued silver-rupee coins from the Calcutta mint for the settlements of Bengal and North India on the pattern of Mughal silver coinage from the Murshidabad mint. These Mughal patterns were stopped in 1834 when the new English sovereign Queen Victoria became empress.

Between 1835 and 1947, uniform coinage in various metals, including silver, were minted from Calcutta and Bombay for the British settlements in India. The British Crown took over the reign of India from the East India Company in 1858.

A new series of silver coins were issued in 1862 on which the figure of Queen Victoria is engraved. In 1877, she became Empress of India, after which silver one-rupee coins with her profile and the

Below: (left) *Reverse of Shah Alam's rupee of his fourth regnal year, bearing the Surat mint name;* ***(centre and right)*** *East India Company silver coin issued in the name of Mughal emperor Shah Alam II from Farrukhabad mint, 19th century; with a flower motif on the reverse*

Left and right: *One-rupee silver coin issued by the British empire, with the profile of Queen Victoria on the obverse and the denmination 'One Rupee' inscribed in the Roman script on the reverse, 19th century*

Below: *Silver tanka struck by Bengal sultan Azam Shah (1382–1384)*

Facing Page: ***(top)*** *Silver rupee issued by Sardar Singh of Bikaner in the name of Queen Victoria, 1917;* ***(centre)*** *Reverse side of Bengal Sultan Azam Shah coin;* ***(bottom)*** *Issued in the name of Shah Alam II, this Indo-French coin was minted in the 18th century*

inscription `Empress' around the border were produced. In the silver one-rupee coin pictured here, 'Ek Rupaiya' is inscribed on the reverse side, and the name of the East India Company.

During the reign of George V (AD 1911) silver coins of eight annas, four annas and two annas were issued. During the period of George VI, the minting of silver coinage in India decreased and was subsequently discontinued altogether. The two World Wars shattered the British and world economies completely. In place of gold and silver, coins were made of copper, bronze, nickel and other alloy metals in India, reflecting the downfall in the economic condition of the country.

SILVER UTILITY ITEMS

From the excavated findings of a silver vessel from Mohenjodaro (Pakistan) and a tiara strip from Kunal (Haryana, India), both from the Harappan period (c. 2500–1800 BC), it is evident that silver was used in ancient India to make items for everyday use. Excavations in Taxila (now in Pakistan) also yielded several silver utensils, vessels and plates, which are on display at the gallery of the National Museum, New Delhi. Later evidence, such as literary references and miniature painting depictions, also testified to the fact that silver was used to make various objects.

Utility items that are also artefacts can be made out of textiles, ivory, wood, stone, silver and other metals and may be plain or decorated with designs and embellishments. There are two types of metal – prime metal and alloy metal. Silver is a prime metal and Indian craftsmen have demonstrated great skill in moulding it to create everyday silverware. Utility objects are shaped into human and animal figures, using various techniques, such as engraving, chasing, damascening, enamelling, repoussé and filigree. Utility items such as nut-cutters, lime (for *paan*) boxes, *huqqa, paandaan, itardaan*, sprinklers and lampstands were made in Delhi, Kashmir, Punjab, Benaras, Agra, Lucknow, Jaipur, Bidar, Kutch, Kerala, Bengal, Assam and Tamil Nadu. Apart from simply shaped utensils, skilled artists also made delicate vessels shaped into bird, animal and human figures, both for domestic use and for religious rituals, displaying their creativity.

The finest silver utility items were made by artists of Kashmir and Punjab. Kashmir's production of samovars and *surahis* (water vessels), with heavy gold plating on silver, is well known. The designs engraved

Facing Page:
Itardaan *(perfume box) containing an array of scent bottles; in golden polished silver, embellished with floral motifs and geometrical patterns in low relief, 20th century*

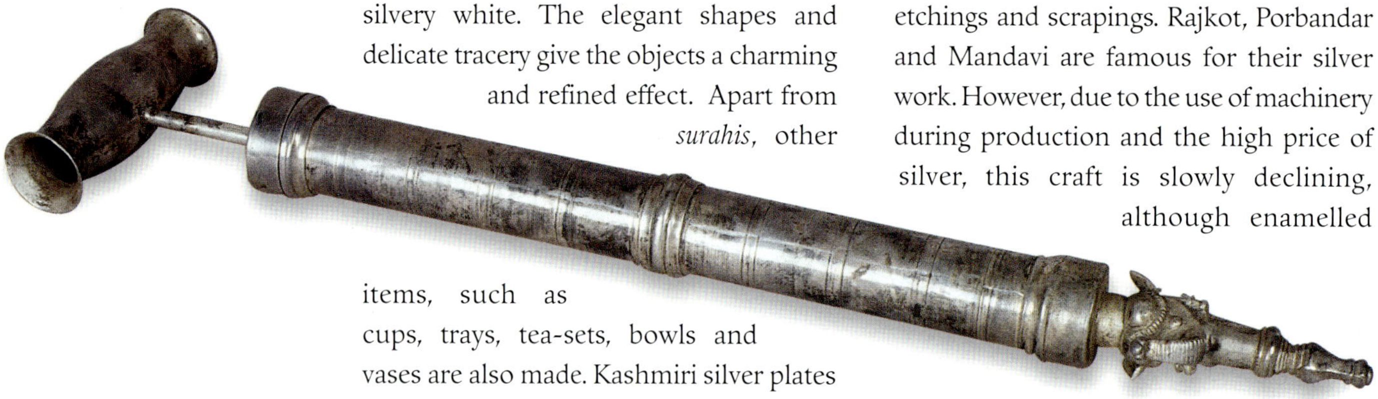

through the gilt to expose the silver underneath form exquisite patterns in silvery white. The elegant shapes and delicate tracery give the objects a charming and refined effect. Apart from *surahis,* other items, such as cups, trays, tea-sets, bowls and vases are also made. Kashmiri silver plates are also well known for their intricate and fine repoussè work in flat relief. Common designs on these plates are *kalka* (resembling paisley motifs) patterns, rosettes and the *chinar* leaf pattern.

In Leh and Ladakh, silver utility objects are created in the Lhasa style, which usually incorporates a large dragon figure. An entire village of silversmiths near Leh is famous for its superb craftsmanship, producing beautiful silver cups, bowls, vessels, plates and tea-pots. Kashmiri artists are renowned for their intricate work, while the Ladakh patterns are bolder and studded with coral and turquoise.

Western India also boasts of a tradition in silverware, a craft still practised by using traditional designs and methods. The repoussè work of Kutch is well known the world over and silver objects like jewellery boxes, *sindoordaani*, rosewater sprinklers, wall screens and *huqqa* stands are manufactured and sold as gift pieces. Thin silver plates are lightly embossed with soft etchings and scrapings. Rajkot, Porbandar and Mandavi are famous for their silver work. However, due to the use of machinery during production and the high price of silver, this craft is slowly declining, although enamelled utility articles are still in demand in the major markets of India. Traders from Rajkot, Jamnagar and Bhuj export enamelled silverware to the Middle East and other foreign markets. The modern craft of engine-turning work on silver, practised in Porbandar and Jamnagar, involves shaping the article by hand and making zigzag patterns with the help of a special machine, equipped with grooved plates. A range of highly polished picture frames and cigar and cigarette cases are made using this technique. In the Kutch area, utility items are made out of the silver bar but in Baroda, silver articles are made by first covering wooden objects with a thin silver plate, which is then gently and skilfully hammered until the metal takes the shape of the woodcarving, giving the article substance. Rajasthan also has a tradition of silverware and various utility

Above:
Pichkari *(syringe) made of silver, the tip of the nozzle shaped like an elephant's trunk, 20th century, Rajasthan*

objects are made there. The work is similar to that of Gujarat, but Rajasthan's traditional patterns and motifs are still employed.

In Bengal, hunting and jungle scenes and rural landscapes are the favoured motifs. These are worked on frosted silver surfaces, producing a subdued yet rich effect. This work has become fairly popular, and objects made by using this technique are also being created in other parts of the country now.

Apart from silver engraving, etching and enamelling, another kind of silver workmanship, known as the Ganga–Jamuna technique, became popular around the late eighteenth and early nineteenth centuries in North India. Ganga symbolizes whiteness, whereas Jamuna represents deep blue. The erstwhile rulers of Awadh (present-day Lucknow and its surrounding areas) had a great fascination for this technique and metal objects such as *huqqa*s, boxes, *aftaba*s (water vessels) and pitchers embellished with gold and silver, were decorated using this technique.

The Mughal emperors influenced the nawabs and provincial rulers of India who began to live in luxury. Various *karkhanas* (workshops) run by nawabs became production centres for utilitarian objects.

Below:
Deities moulded in exquisite repoussé workmanship, framed by floral and leaf patterns, embellish this small rectangular silver box used to keep items for ritualistic worship, 19th century, South India

Below:
Bidri abkhwura *(water container) in metal alloy and silver inlay, with floral patterns on the outer surface and fine calligraphy on the interior, 19th century, Hyderabad*

Facing Page:
Decorated with geometric patterns in silver enamelling, this small vessel, with a spout in the shape of an animal's head, is used as a kahwa *(spiced tea) pot, 19th century, Himachal Pradesh*

Some common objects used for day-to-day living and on ceremonial occasions are: *abkhwura* (water container), *aftaba* (water vessel), *alam* (staff), *chauri*-handle (fly-whisk handle), cups, *huqqa* (smoking pipe), *husnadaan* (betel-and-perfume box), inkpot and pencase, jewellery box, *mir-i-farsh (*carpet weight), nut-cutter, *paandaan* (betel container), perfume box, rosewater sprinkler, *sailabchi* (wash-basin), samovars, screens, spittoons, *surahi* and *surmadaani* (collyrium container) and decorative objects including camels, elephants and *haudas* (elephant seats).

ABKHWURA

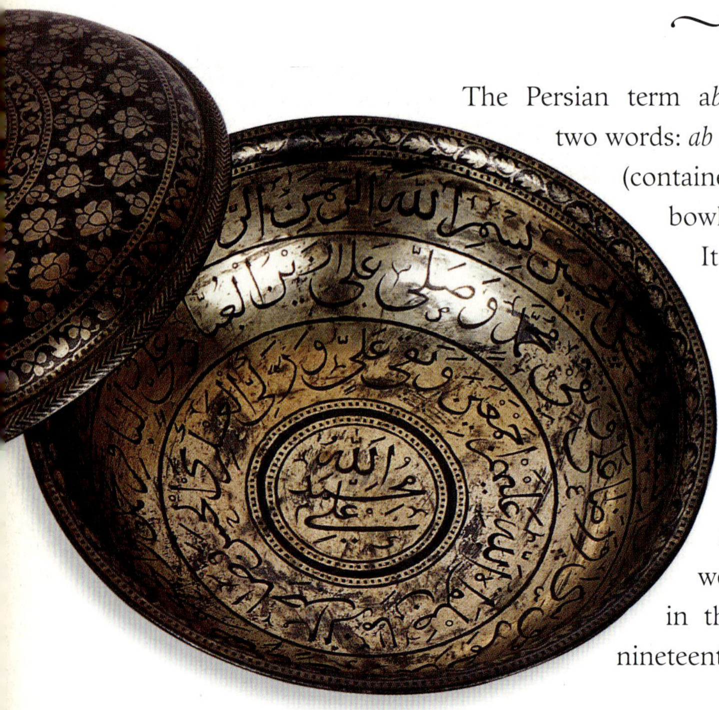

The Persian term *abkhwura* comprises two words: *ab* (water) and *khwura* (container), and means a bowl for drinking water. It is believed that drinking water from such a bowl will protect the drinker from evil and also impart extra strength. *Bidri abkhwuras* were in great demand in the eighteenth and nineteenth centuries in the Deccan region. Skilfully crafted *bidri abkhwuras* were ornate and had slightly raised circular bases. The outer surface of the bowls were decorated with various patterns in the shape of flowers such as poppies, lotuses or roses, while the inside had circular calligraphy and verses from the Holy Koran in Arabic in the Naksh script. Such *abkhwuras* were popular utensils and became essential components of dowries in the Deccan. The original centre of this artwork is Bidar but it also took root in the eastern part of India (Murshidabad and Purnia) in the late twentieth century.

AFTABA

Ab means water and *aftaba* refers to an ewer, a water vessel. *Aftabas* were generally used to pour water when washing hands into a *sailabchi* (portable basin). Since *aftabas* were used in living rooms, they were crafted with plenty of embellishments, intricate designs and innovative handles. Around the eighteenth to nineteenth centuries, numerous kinds of *aftaba* were manufactured in different sizes and shapes but the most common shape was circular. Artisans also used various materials such as ceramic, silver, brass, bronze or copper and a variety of

Below:
Hand-shaped alam *(religious standard) in silver with a glittering golden polish, North India*

Right:
Detail of the alam *showing the silhouette of a mosque within a frame in the shape of a heart-shaped leaf*

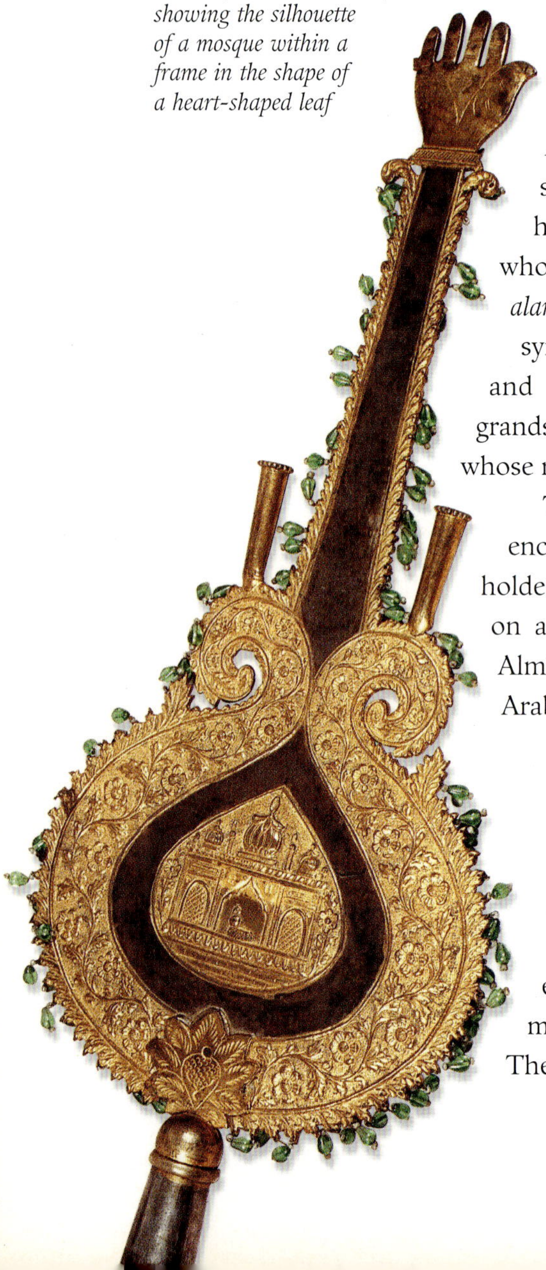

*aftaba*s can be seen in various museums in India and abroad.

ALAM

Alam (meaning sacred) is the staff carried by a leader in the procession during the Shia Muslim festival of Muharram. *Alams* are made in different shapes like a *panja* (hand), a human form or a fish. The person who holds the *alam* is known as an *alam bardar*. The *panja*-shaped *alam* symbolizes the hands of Hassan and Hussain, the two martyred grandsons of Prophet Mohammad in whose memory Muharram is observed. The *panja* is decorated with encrustation work and has a conical holder at the base, which can be fixed on a stick. Verses in praise of the Almighty were also inscribed in the Arabic or the Persian script.

CHAURI

A *chauri* was a fly-whisk used in courts by attendants of emperors to wave over the monarch as he sat on the throne. The tradition of using *chauri*s is very old and has been mentioned in various texts – the Didarganj Yakshi (famous sculpture of a nature deity of the Mauryan period (third century BC) – is depicted holding a *chauri*. A fly-whisk consists of two parts: the hair that composes the fan and the handle to which it is attached. Yak or other animal hair is the favoured material and the handle is made of ivory, wood or silver. Handles made of silver were adorned whisks used by royalty and for religious or ceremonial activities.

CUP

Mughal emperor Jahangir was fond of jade and several jade cups were made during his reign; some of these cups with his name

engraved on them are displayed in museum collections in India and abroad. These cups were actually small bowls used for drinking wine. Later, during the British period, silver cups became fashionable and were used to drink tea and coffee. They were either enamel painted or decorated with engravings of flora and fauna and reflected the artistic skill of metal carvers.

HUQQA

In India, tobacco-smoking through a *huqqa* (Urdu), *qalian* (Persian), *gud-gudi* (Hindi) or the hubble-bubble became popular from the seventeenth century onwards. Around the fifteenth–sixteenth century AD, the Portuguese brought tobacco-smoking to India and *huqqa*s became a common feature during Jahangir's reign (1605–1627) and onwards. Around the eighteenth–nineteenth century, the *huqqa* became fashionable, and this trend was reflected in several Pahari, Deccan and Rajasthani miniature paintings in which emperors have been depicted smoking *huqqa*s. Emperors and nawabs would employ a *huqqadar* whose work involved filling the *huqqa*s and other related work, such as cleaning and maintaining them. Smoking *huqqa*s was to become prevalent among men and women of all walks of life. Several Mughal miniature paintings also depict *huqqas* and a variety of these pipes in different materials, including metal, jade, glass, stone, brass and silver, are housed in different museums in India and abroad, indicating its rich tradition. Silverware artists of North India have made innovations in the shapes and sizes of *huqqas*; coconut-shaped, circular and bell-shaped *huqqas* are the most popular. However, artists custom-made *huqqas* with bases in almond and bird shapes and often in the form of a female. Sometimes these objects, especially those made in the *bidri* technique, were decorated with flora and fauna designs, chequered patterns or even state insignia. The National Museum has a *bidri huqqa* on display, depicting the state insignia of the Nawab of Awadh.

A *huqqa* consists of five main parts. The first part is the base vessel used for holding water, the second is a hollow stem connecting the neck of the *huqqa* base with the *chillum,* the third part, which holds the substance that is being smoked. The fourth part is a long tube ending in the fifth part, the mouth-piece through which the smoke is inhaled.

HUSNADAAN

Husnadaan is the term used for a container to store prepared betel-nuts

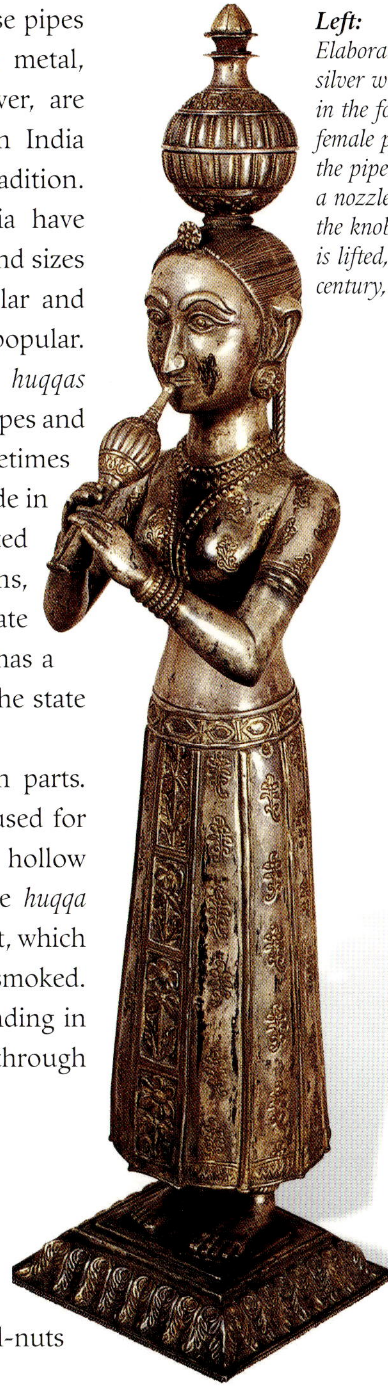

Left:
Elaborately curved silver wine bottle in the form of a female piper, with the pipe acting as a nozzle when the knob at the top is lifted, 20th century, Rajasthan

Right:
Elongated silver pencase decorated with floral and zigzag patterns and attached to a crescent-shaped inkpot with thick chains, 19th century, Rajasthan

Facing Page:
Melon-shaped silver gagar *(water vessel) ornamented with a stylized floral creeper and a European-style flower vase engraved in its centre, 20th century, North India*

and perfume buds. *Husna,* an Urdu word, means beauty, while *daan* means container. Traditionally, betel-nuts were a part of the paraphernalia used for beautification because of the colour they impart and was often required at the final stage of make-up. Craftsmen therefore designed *husnadaans* with two distinct divisions, one to store betel-nuts and the other for perfume buds or other items used as make-up.

INKPOT AND PENCASE

During the Mughal period, the art of calligraphy and painting flourished. Artists were therefore inspired to create holders for pens, ink, brushes and pigments. Silver inkpots and pencases were also made by the artists of the time. One beautiful silver inkpot attached to a pencase worked with floral creepers and zigzag patterns is in the collection at the National Museum and is an example of the silver craft of the nineteenth century. The small crescent-shaped inkpot is made of camel skin, which was popular in Rajasthan around this time. A small flower-shaped lid and a little rectangular base enhances its form. Several Rajasthani miniature paintings illustrate inkpots and pencases.

JEWELLERY BOX

A jewellery box is an essential component of a woman's make-up kit. Understanding the demand for it, silverware artisans made different kinds of jewellery boxes for women. The usual shape is rectangular but the box is sometimes circular. These boxes were also used to keep valuables in, and were beautifully painted, carved or inlayed with motifs. A variety of floral patterns, human figures, and architectural, boat and cart motifs have been used to embellish jewellery boxes, employing the techniques of enamel painting, repoussé or engraving and golden-wire inlay work.

An intricately carved jewellery box, with bird and floral patterns all over the surface and resting on an elegantly crafted elephant-shaped stand, is displayed in the National Museum, New Delhi. An excellent example of the craftsmanship of the nineteenth century of western India, its entire upper surface is carved in ogee arches against a backdrop of floral patterns. The arches depict a peacock and parrot alternating with a European-style floral creeper strip between the body and lid and latticework strips run along the edge.

MIR-I-FARSH

Mir-i-farsh is a Persian word, meaning minister (*mir*) of the floor (*farsh*) and is the term used for a carpet weight. *Mir-i-farsh* were used as posts for beds and served as weights for floor coverings, especially embroidered cotton and silk *farshi* (floor spreads). Pahari miniature paintings from the seventeenth–nineteenth centuries as well as paintings from the Deccan and Rajasthan depict *farshi*. *Mir-i-farsh* are usually small but heavy. Most have square or circular bases with heavy domes fixed on them. Since these small objects are

Facing Page:
Silver perfume box with floral gem-studded patterns in fine filigree workmanship

Below:
Detail of the perfume box, highlighting the gold polish on the silver surface

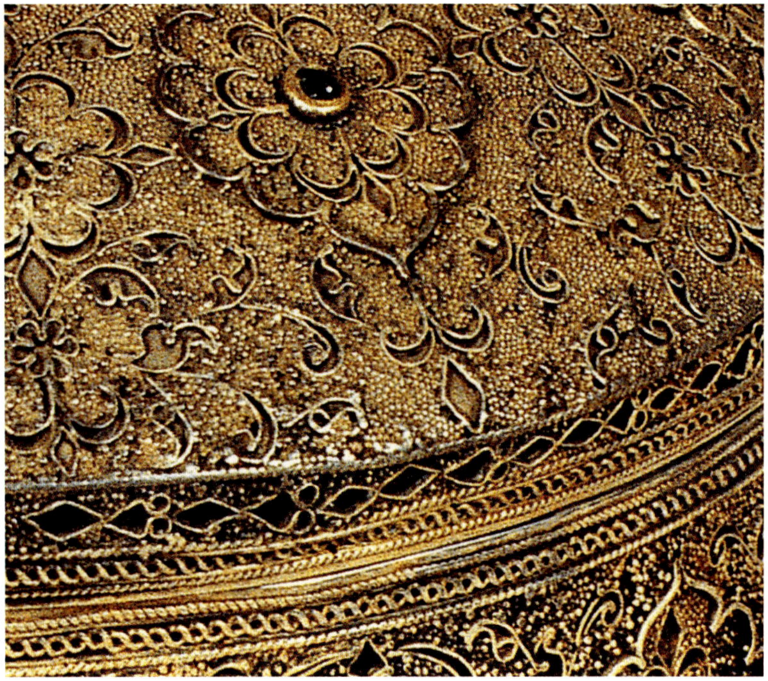

Below:
Delicate filigree workmanship adorns this silver perfume box set in a flower-shaped container on a tray; each exquisitely carved flower holds a fragrance-filled cotton ball in the centre, 19th century, Orissa

Below:
Silver gold-polished tray with small containers to keep cotton wicks soaked in itar *or perfume*

Below:
Dome-shaped paandaan *(betel-roll container) decorated with bands of floral and fish motifs; the fish is a symbol of fertility associated with* paan*, a symbol of love, 20th century, North India*

generally centrepieces, they are heavily embellished. The dome shape is sometimes worked into flower or bud shapes.

Bidri carpet weights have circular bases and dome-shaped upper portions with both pieces joined together. The knobs are often decorated with floral patterns. Sometimes, the entire carpet weight is decorated with poppy-flower or petal patterns, with the edges worked in the *aftabi* technique with silver.

NUT-CUTTERS

Traditionally, betel-nuts first cracked by nut-cutters, were then wrapped in betel leaves and chewed. Nut-cutters were most commonly made of brass but silver nut-cutters were used on special occasions. Made in various shapes including horses, lions or parrots, the most interesting piece is a nut-cutter (displayed in the Raja Dinkar Kelkar Museum, Pune) in the shape of an amorous couple, which has a small curved blade in the form of a male and female and decorated handles in the shape of legs. The male figure is depicted in a passionate embrace with the female, who is in a stance of equal adoration. The jewellery and costumes have been worked with encrustation work, reflecting the culture and fashion of the time. When animal shapes have been used for nut-cutters, the cutting blade is usually in the shape of the body of the animal.

PAANDAAN

The practice of chewing betel on important occasions is considered auspicious in India. Apart from ceremonies, betel-chewing was also a part of day-to-day activity; it became customary to chew betel leaf with lime, betel-nut and other accompanying ingredients after every meal. It is also believed to help digestion.

Around the sixth–seventh century the betel-roll, known as *paan,* was introduced and it slowly became an integral part of Hindu rituals and social conventions. By the fourteenth–fifteenth century, it was enjoyed by all, whether rich or poor, rural or urban, men or women. This custom encouraged artisans to create betel boxes or *paandaan* to keep the betel leaf, lime, *katha* and nut, ingredients in the betel-roll, in a container. Most *paandaan* have four or five small divisions, and each may be further partitioned. Sometimes, bigger *paandaan* carry smaller containers, to keep separate ingredients. Square, rectangular and circular *paandaan* are the most common. Since *paan* was customary in North Indian weddings in the eighteen–nineteenth century, silver *paandaan*, worked with various techniques including repoussé, filigree and engraving, became popular.

PERFUME BOX

The use of perfume or *itar* by men and women after bathing is an ancient Indian practice. Vedic, Buddhist and Sanskrit literature refer to a variety of flowers and types of wood (sandalwood, for instance) that were used for making *itar* by Indians of that period. To store a variety of fragrances, artisans made perfume boxes or *itardaan* in ivory, silver or brass. These boxes were generally circular, octagonal or rectangular with partitions made to hold small bottles.

A perfume box is usually a small silver rectangular box with twelve small bottles with lids, in which perfume is kept. A silver sheet with twelve cutouts is placed inside the box, so that the narrow bottles can stand upright. Claw-shaped small legs are the stands; a clasp and a handle on the top indicate that the box can be used as a vanity case. The outer surface of the box is often embellished with a floral creeper in worked in repoussé.

ROSEWATER SPRINKLER

While perfumes are for individual use, rosewater is used in large gatherings – it is sprinkled to freshen the air during social gatherings or religious functions. Small water vessels with long necks and circular bases hold the rosewater. The tip of the vessel has small holes through which the scented water is sprinkled. Rosewater is the main perfumed water used on special occasions, hence the vessel is named after it, but other fragrances are also used.

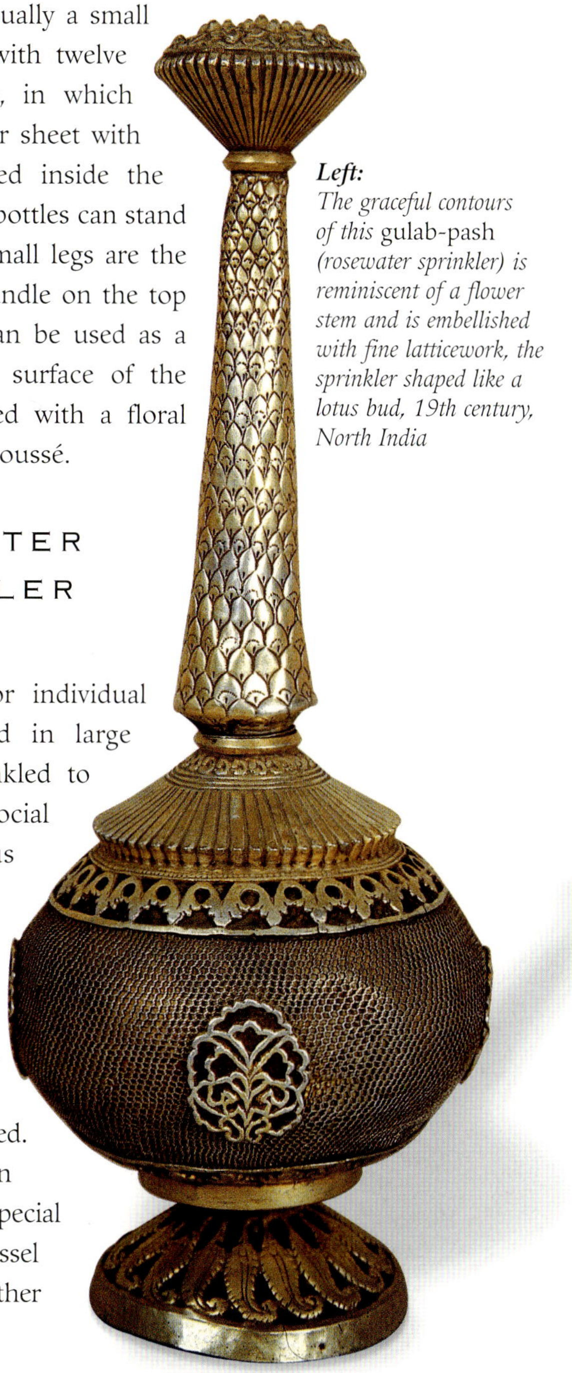

Left:
The graceful contours of this gulab-pash *(rosewater sprinkler) is reminiscent of a flower stem and is embellished with fine latticework, the sprinkler shaped like a lotus bud, 19th century, North India*

Left:
Silver butter lamp used in Buddhist prayer rooms to keep a flame burning during worship, Ladakh

Facing Page:
Resting on a small ide *(circular ring) is this curved* matka *(water vessel) enhanced by ornately carved figures of Lord Krishna (Laddugopal – with a butter bowl) and a* mridang-vadika *(female playing a drum), 20th century, North India*

Right:
Candle-holder in the graceful shape of a lotus flower with leaves and held up by stems; it stands on a tray formed like a flower in exquisite bidri *workmanship, 19th century, Hyderabad*

SAILABCHI

A *sailabchi* is a washbasin often used inside a room along with an *aftaba*. The upper portion of a *sailabchi* is usually embellished with floral or leaf motifs; it has a flared plate-shaped portion, while the base is globular. *Bidri sailabchi* inlayed with silver were favoured in the Deccan region.

SAMOVAR

A samovar is a vessel used as a kettle in Kashmir for the preparation of *kahva*, a spiced tea flavoured with ingredients such as cardamom and saffron. The tradition of drinking this tea is indigenously Central Asian and in Kashmir, the vessel is modified and decorated in the local style. A samovar generally has a very elegant rounded body, a small, curved spout, a handle and a base. These vessels are beautifully decorated on the surface with Kashmiri patterns like the *kalka* (paisley motifs used in *jamawar* shawls) patterns, floral creepers and a variety of flora and fauna. Samovars made of tin are for daily use whereas silver ones are used on special social occasions.

SCREEN

A screen (folding wall) is used in a room when a temporary partition is needed. It consists of four or five door-leafs, which are attached to each other with hinges so that the screen can be folded. The use of screens is popular in the Islamic tradition and can be seen in miniature paintings. They are generally made of wood and are decorated in different styles; they may be inlayed with ivory or simply engraved and covered with silver sheets. In western India, wood is often covered with silver.

SPITTOON

An essential utensil for use with *paan* or betel is a spittoon, used for spitting betel waste in. Known as *ugaldaan*, the usual shape of spittoons, especially *bidri*ware, is of two bell-shaped bowls placed one upon another so that they are joined at their centres and face opposite directions. The lower bowl works as a pedestal, while the upper bowl is used as a basin to spit out the betel waste. Since *bidri* objects were given as part of a dowry, large numbers of *bidri ugaldaan* were made in the Deccan. These were artistically decorated with flora and fauna patterns, the silver inlay on the black metal making a striking contrast.

SURAHI

Surahi, vessels for storing wine and water, were initially imported from Iran and went through a number of transformations in India, changing from tall, elegant vase-like shapes to those with squatter and more rounded bodies, with the neck ending in a spout, known as an *aftaba*.

Surahis were made in precious materials such as gold, silver, jade, ceramics and metal. Craftsmen of Rajasthan, Gujarat, Delhi, Himachal Pradesh, Kashmir and Punjab specialize in making silver *surahis*. These vessels are circular or elongated and regional styles of engraving, repoussé, *bidri* and enamel art are worked on them.

SURMADAANI

Surma or *kajal* (collyrium) is one of the most basic cosmetics in an Indian woman's toiletry. *Surma* or *kajal* containers are known as *surmadaani*. These small containers are made of different materials, shapes and sizes. Brass and silver are preferred, in pot or pillar shapes. Sometimes the container has a stick attached to it, which is used to put collyrium in the eyes.

SHAMADAAN

Shamadaan (lampshade) comprises *shama* (meaning light) and *daan* (meaning container). During the Mughal period, the tradition of covering lamps became

Right:
Long silver box decorated with floral and zigzag patterns, used to keep cosmetics such as surma *(collyrium)*

fashionable, and the *shamadaan* came into use. Made in various shapes such as pillars or domes, they were highly decorative.

DECORATIVE OBJECTS

Apart from utilitarian objects, Indian artists created decorative items as well. They were often made to order, therefore their sizes and shapes varied vastly.

CAMEL

A couple seated on a camel, which rests on an oval pedestal, is in the collection of the National Museum, New Delhi. The apparent movement of the camel and the depiction of the couple that face one another in a romantic stance is executed in an artistic manner and is reminiscent of the legendary love story of Dhola-Maru of Rajasthan. The couple is depicted in Rajasthani attire; the female is in a *lehnga-choli-odhani* (long skirt, blouse and scarf) and the male has long moustaches and wears a *dhoti-jama-pagri* (loin cloth and turban), both holding a *surahi* (water or wine container) and cup. The pedestal has encrusted floral designs, while the camel has been worked in the repoussé technique on the wooden base. It is a beautiful example of the silver craftsmanship of twentieth-century western India.

ELEPHANT AND SEAT

On display in the National Museum is a pair of decorative elephants, an excellent example of Rajasthani craftsmanship of the nineteenth and twentieth centuries.

Below:
Flexible silver container for spices, paan *or cosmetics in the streamlined contours of a fish, 20th century, Bengal*

Facing Page:
Ornamental silver top with a tiny nailed tip on which it rotates; perched on the rounded upper part is an elegant parrot, 20th century, western India

The elephants are sculpted along with a *mahavat* (mahout) and *chauri*-bearer (person who bears the fly-whisk), and are adorned with necklaces, anklets, and *hathi-ki-jhool* (elephant trappings). The *mahavat* and *chauri*-bearer wear Rajasthani costumes along with the typical Rajasthani head-gear. Made of wood and covered with a silver sheet, it has been worked in the repoussé technique and is an excellent example of the decorative style practised by western Indian artists..

Elephants have always been the subject of great interest to the people of India – they have been used by the common man and royalty, in times of both war and peace. An elephant-seat or *hauda* would be placed on the back of the elephant and the king, along with the *mahavat* and *chauri*-bearer, would sit under the umbrella (*chhatra*).The elephants were also decorated with *hathi-ki-jhool* (elephant trappings), including extravagant head-gear, necklaces and anklets. Such ceremonial processions are taken out even today in Rajasthan, Kerala and Mysore, especially during festivals.

*Aftaba*s, *alams*, *huqqa*s, *paandaan*s and other containers, screens, silver plates and a plethora of other silver objects are in daily use among the elite but most people use them only on special occasions. Many of these exquisite objects were custom-made for those who could afford them, but in general, people buy silverware available in the market and the tradition continues to this day.

RELIGIOUS AND CEREMONIAL SILVER OBJECTS

India has been known for its religious thought and spirituality for over 5,000 years. In common with the practice of nature worship in the early religions of Egypt and Greece, Indian religious rituals involved obeisance to nature. The Indian way of life, traditionally known as *Sanatana Dharma* (immortal duty), was governed by moral values and duties. Hinduism was polytheistic in its earlier stages, but the gods Shiva and Vishnu and goddess Durga became more prominent later. After the sixth century BC, Buddhism, Jainism, Sikhism, Islam, Christianity and Zoroastrianism also made forays into India and took root.

According to Hinduism, there are three ways of attaining liberation: through *jnana* (knowledge), *karma* (action) and *bhakti* (devotion). Through *bhakti*, worshippers have a personal communion with the gods. There are two kinds of *bhakti*; the first involves *dhyana* (concentration) while the second subscribes to *mantra* (verses in the praise of God) and elaborate rituals. Devotees of the *mantra* form are the patrons of religious art. Images of gods and goddesses, clothes and ornaments for the divinities and a wide variety of accessories for the rituals, comprising of thrones, lamps and even musical instruments to accompany hymns sung in the praise of gods during prayer make up the gamut of silver votive objects.

Metal is an important ingredient both for religious and household accessories. Religious metal images are installed not only in temples and the homes of the wealthy, but also in simple shrines and humble homes. Metal talismans are worn in the belief that they ward off evil and disease. Indian metalware includes images, utensils and jewellery made in accordance with the tenets of the

Facing Page:
Elaborately carved and ornamented double-storeyed silver incense-burner crowned with a star within a crescent moon.

Shilpashastras, ancient treatises that enumerate the tenets of architecture. Wealthy people fabricated religious and ceremonials objects in gold while the middle class, including religious organizations, used silver religious objects.

IMAGES OF GODS AND GODDESSES

The *Shilpashastras* contain detailed descriptions of Hindu gods and goddesses and most images of divinities are manufactured on the basis of these texts. Seven materials are prescribed, one of which is silver. It further mentions the advantage of using these materials for making images of deities. Silver statues of gods and goddesses are supposed to bring wealth to the worshipper, therefore the seat, umbrella and palanquin of the deity, the temple chariot, and doors and dome of the temple are either made of silver or of wax covered with silver.

SILVER TEMPLES

Although most temples are made of brick and stone, some Indian temples are entirely constructed in silver, or their doors, lintels and windows are coated with silver. In Rajasthan, Hindu or Jain temples made of silver belonged to royal families of ancient lineage or big business houses. One example, which seems to have been part of a temple from western India, probably Gujarat, is displayed in the decorative art gallery of the National Museum, New Delhi. The temple has doors, the upper frame of a doorway and three small *shikharas* (spires). The central upper portion of the doorway-frame depicts the goddess Saraswati seated on a lotus pedestal playing the *veena* (stringed musical instrument).

Apart from western India, the silver temple tradition exists in South India where temples are sheathed lavishly with silver and beautifully embellished with foliage designs and depictions of stories from the scriptures. Massive silver doors and windows display fine workmanship with a profusion of traditional motifs such as Gajalakshmi images with conch-shell motifs, or Shiva and Parvati, seated on Nandi (bull). Silver temples also depict images of Mahishasuramardini (goddess

Durga) or Krishna flanked by his consorts. Goddesses Shridevi and Bhudevi are also engraved or worked in repoussé. Sometimes silver is polished with gold and studded with semi-precious stones.

GHATA (SACRED POT)

Traditionally, a priest or his attendant would bring fresh water in a *ghata* (sacred pot) either from a river, pond or well as part of the ritual of worship in a temple. These pots would be made of silver, brass or copper. Priests or attendants would fill the water in the silver pot and recite Sanskrit verses in praise of Lord Varun (god of water) and pray for salvation. The silver water pots were embellished with floral patterns and engraved or embossed with religious symbols like the *shree vatsa*, conch shells, lotus and *tilak* symbols. Most silver water pots were donated by royal families or wealthy landlords in order to pay homage to the deities.

SPOON

Chammacha, silver spoons, are used to offer *arghya* (water to wash the hands), *padya* (water offered to the deity), and *achamanya* (water offered to sip and rinse the mouth) and for distributing sanctified water to the worshippers. Silver spoons are made with long handles, with large artistically designed tips decorated with floral patterns, serpent hoods, and the *sudarshan charka* (wheel of Vishnu).

SPOUTED JUG

Silver or metal spouted jugs, also known as *aftaba,* are used to hold water during various ceremonies in temples. Priests use the *aftaba* to sanctify flowers and other objects of worship. The vessel's spout is made in several shapes, including those of lions or crocodiles. The jugs are often carved with insignias of the gods Vishnu, Shiva and Ganesha and the

Facing Page:
Silver image of the popular elephant god Ganesha in the bhikshatan mudra *(begging posture symbolic of a saint), holding an umbrella and a begging bowl*

Below:
Small silver spoon with a circular scoop and a long handle with a conical tip, designed to protect the user from heat in rituals involving fire, such as sprinkling ghee *(clarified butter) on a pyre*

Facing Page:
High relief work in repoussé on this silver glass portrays Hanuman, the monkey god, holding a mountain aloft in one hand and a gada *(mace) on the other, surrounded by a graceful floral creeper band, 20th century, Rajasthan*

Below:
Details of the silver glass on facing page, showing a close-up of the Hanuman figure and the floral creeper band above the arch

goddess Durga. In Kashmir, silver spouted jugs are made in the Ganga–Jamuna style. *Bidri* spouted vessels are also popular.

PEETHA (TRIPOD)

One of the most important objects used in religious rituals in the temples of India is the *peetha*, a tripod consisting of a large circular plate with five vessels called *panchapatra* (*panch* means five, *patra* means vessel) placed in front of the deity, close to the priest's seat and used for worship. The deities are placed on these seats for ritual baths; there are certain prescribed rules about the seat and posture of the priest during worship. The legs of the tripod are often shaped like those of an elephant to create a solid base, but some tripods are tortoise-shaped because according to Hindu philosophy, the earth rests on a tortoise's back.

DHARA PATRA (ABLUTION VESSEL)

Traditionally, it is believed that water should continuously flow during the deities' ritual baths – metal-workers, therefore, created the *dhara patra* (ablution vessel). Lord Shiva is also known as Abhishekpriya (one who likes ablutions) and so ablution vessels are found only in temples dedicated to Shiva. Hung directly above the *shivalinga*, these vessels have a single mouth-opening. River water or clean tap water filled in it drips over the *linga* in a continuous stream to propitiate Lord Shiva. Generally, these ablution vessels are conical in shape and made of silver, and have carved and embossed decorations with Shaivite patterns. Artists have also made these vessels in the shape of the bull Nandi, Shiva and his consort Parvati's vehicle.

SHANKHA (CONCH SHELL)

The conch shell, obtained from river- or sea-beds is considered one of the most auspicious objects used during rituals in Hindu temples. Hindus believe that the sound of the conch shell is holy and will ward off misfortunes. The formations of a conch shell are varied and are classified into male, female and hermaphrodite. Well-shaped as it is, craftsmen enhance its beauty, by coating its head and tail portions in silver or gold plating, thus protecting it from damage. In Hindu families, all religious and auspicious functions start after the conch shell is blown. During ancient times, the blowing of the conch shell was the announcement of war, heralding battles to come.

KAMANDALA (WATER POT)

Kamandala is the water pot used by *sadhus* (priests) for their personal use. They are usually made of herbal wood but saints and seers like the Shankarcharyas of the various *peetham* (religious centres) use a silver *kamandala.* These are round or conical shaped with or without lids, but with a handle and spout. The surfaces of *kamandalas* are intricately carved, depicting stories and scenes from the scriptures,

such as *Dasavatara* (the ten incarnations of Vishnu), or with the depiction of various aspects of the goddesses Kali, Durga and Parvati. Islamic *kamandalas*, known as *kushkul,* are decorated with verses from the Koran, usually in beautiful calligraphy.

PANKHA (FAN)

Traditionally, the image of a deity is treated as a King of kings in every religion. Fans, fly-whisks, mirrors, insignias and *patakas* (religious flags or banners) are part of the paraphernalia of royalty. Fans are generally made of grass or large palm leaves, bamboo chips and colourful cloth. But in prosperous temples, such as in South India, fans are sometimes made in silver, with oyster-shaped handles, beautifully decorated with flower patterns around the edges. Fans in Jain temples and Sikh *gurudwaras* are embellished with depictions of the deities.

CHAMAR (FLY-WHISK)

The fly-whisk or *chamar* used to fan the divinities is made of the tail hair of the *kasturi mriga* (musk deer) or from the hair of the yak. The handle of the fly-whisk has a long metal rod made of various materials. Besides silver, which is the most popular, handles are also made of brass, ivory or of bamboo reed. The upper portion of the handle has a cup, used to attach the long hairs, while the tip usually has a roundel. These rods are often adorned with beautiful engravings or etchings. Devotees use fly-whisks in temples, *gurudwaras* and in religious processions to fan the deities and religious books, as well as the seers and saints.

Facing Page:
Seven triangular panels form this religious bandhavar *(banner) covered with symbols.*

Left:
Fan made of strands of silver wire

Below:
Fine silver wire has been woven to create these beautiful fly-whisks with latticework fringes

MIRROR

Mirrors are important religious utility items in temples. In Shiva temples, mirrors are placed behind Nandi, so that Shiva can view his *vahana* (vehicle) through the mirror. In South India, priests place mirrors outside the *garbha-griha* (sanctum-sanctorum of a temple) to catch the early rays of the sun and reflect it on the *shivalinga*. Frames and handles of mirrors were often made of silver.

LANCHANA AND PATAKA (INSIGNIAS AND FLAGS)

Every deity of the Hindu pantheon has certain insignias and flags related to them: the *shankha* (conch shell), *chakra* (wheel), *gada* (mace) and *padma* (lotus)

Above:
Small. colourful fabric bag, finely woven in glittering silver thread, used to keep cosmetics in

Facing Page:
Buddhist symbols adorn this sacred container for religious insignia and books; the projected loops are designed to enable a traveller to clasp it closely to the body

Right: **Right:** *Lavishly embellished with images of deities is this silver temple in the* gopuram *style*

Left:
Double-storeyed octangular lampstand with a door opening into the interior, the delicate latticework allowing light to filter in; it is crowned with a crescent moon

Facing Page:
Silver-polished wooden image of Garuda, Lord Vishnu's vehicle

Below:
Small silver plaque with a folk deity engraved in low relief; such plaques can also be worn as pendants

are Lord Vishnu's attributes, while the *damaru* (small drum), *trishul* (trident), *sarpa* (snake) and Nandi (bull) are associated with Lord Shiva. Apart from Hindu deities, insignias and flags are also used in Buddhist, Jain, Sikh, Christian and even in Islamic ceremonies. Most of these insignias are made of silver and highlight the symbolic form of the divinity. The size of the *pataka* vary according to the occasion; if they are to be used in religious or ceremonial processions they are large and may also be fixed on a wooden rod, whereas if they are to be used within shrines, they are smaller. Insignias are also used in symbolical worship. Many wars in Indian mythology and historical wars were fought under these flags.

FLOWER BASKETS

Deities are adorned by priests and worshippers with flowers, made either into garlands or left loose. Every temple has flower-pots or baskets which are used to collect them. Flower baskets in silver or metal are of varying sizes and shapes; they may be round, octagonal or bowl-shaped with handles, and are decorated using techniques such as embossing, enamelling and filigree. The patterns on baskets vary from flower designs to images of deities.

SHATARI

A *shatari* is a crown-shaped object, usually made of silver, found in Vaishnavite (followers of Vishnu) temples of South India. This elongated cap is placed at the feet of the deity during a religious ceremony. It is composed of two or three tiers and decorated with embossed sacred flowers, designs or insignias. The usual practice in South Indian Vaishnavite temples is for the head priest to place the *shatari* on the head of the devotees when they complete their worship of Vishnu or his incarnations. This act symbolizes the assurance that the devotee will be protected. There are norms prescribed for this ritual; the *shatari* is put five times

Above:
Richly worked Jain manuscript cover divided into fourteen panels, each embellished with the religious symbols of Jainism in high relief

on the head of the *acharyas* (religious teachers), three times for men and once for women.

KUMKUM VESSEL

Special vessels or pots are created by artists to keep vermilion powder in the temples of goddesses Kali, Durga, Parvati, Lakshmi and Vaishnavi. Pots (without lids) or boxes (with lids) are usually made of silver or gold. In temples, the presiding goddess is given a ritual bath every morning before being decorated with flowers, silk and jewellery. Once the embellishment is over, a pinch of vermilion powder is offered to the goddess; this act is performed either 108 times or 1008 times and is accompanied by the recitation of verses in praise of the goddess. Vermilion powder is later distributed to devotees who apply it between the eyebrows or at the centre of the forehead. There are large and small vermilion boxes and a variety of techniques, including enamelling, filigree work, engraving and repoussé, are used to decorate them. Traditionally, every married Hindu woman keeps small vermilion containers, which come in several shapes and sizes, including those of pots, flowers and fish, in a vanity box.

JHOOLA (CRADLE)

The swing ceremony is an important ritual in Hinduism. This is performed at night to put a deity to bed. Followers of Lord Krishna play on the swing on the occasion of the festival of Janamashtami (the birth of Lord Krishna). Cradles are found in every Indian temple; most cradles are made of silver but they can also be made of wood. Wooden swings are decorated either with pigments, mirrors or a silver covering. These are also embellished with designs of foliage and insignias pertaining to the deities. Their sizes also vary, according to the significance of the deity.

DEEP (LAMP)

According to the *Taitariya Brahmana*, a religious treatise, Surya (the sun) and Agni (fire) are the main sources of light; everyone, it says, should pray to the light in the evening. The manufacturing of lamps scaled new heights of excellence under the skilled hands of silver craftsmen. The single-wick lamp from the second century AD and the intricate hanging lamps of today are testimony to their skilled workmanship. South Indian craftsmen further enriched this art by producing exquisite temple lamps. These lamps are of two varieties: lamps used for general illumination and those used in religious rituals. There are several kinds of designs, including multi-tiered lamps, patterned with animal and floral motifs, hanging lamps and ritual lamps in temples made in a variety of materials. Silver lamps, however, remain popular in temples and in households.

Religious festivals in honour of various deities hold an important place in Indian society. These temple festivals add charm and colour to the lives of people, who welcome a change from their daily routine. The *Rathyatra* (chariot festival) at Puri, Orissa, the *Kumbha Mela* (the sacred-pot fair) at Allahabad, Uttar Pradesh, the *Mahamastakabhisheka* of Bahubali, a Jain *Tirthankara* at Shravanbelagola, Karnataka, and the *Brahmotsava* at Tirupati, South India, are some festivals of national importance.

PALAKI (PALANQUIN)

In some temples, figures of deities seated in a *palaki* are taken out in processions

Facing Page:
Silver doorway of a temple dedicated to goddess Saraswati flanked by images of dwarapalas *(guards)*

Below:
Silver canopy of a miniature chariot in delicate workmanship

around the main shrine or within the precincts of a temple. In small temples, the palanquins are simpler, whereas large temples have large, artistically decorated *palaki* made of silver or are gold- plated. Silver palanquins are decorated with a variety of flowers and tassels suspended from silver or gold-plated cups. In a religious procession, the main deity is placed in the richly decorated palanquin and whole-hearted attention is bestowed on the deity.

RATHAS (CHARIOTS)

Installed within most temples of South India are miniature chariots made of wood, some of which are covered with silver plate. They are beautifully decorated with carvings of floral design and depictions of mythological scenes. Precious stones are also embedded in some chariots. On an auspicious day every year, temple deities are taken out in the surrounding areas in decorated chariots and honoured by temple priests. This procession is called *rathayatra* (travel by chariot). Chariot festivals are frequent in Puri, Orissa, and in South India, the Puri *Rathayatra* festival being especially popular and well known. During this festival, people participate in large numbers and are eager to pull the chariot in which the image of the deity is placed. There are several temples in Karnataka and Tamil Nadu, where old wooden chariots are covered with silver and sometimes, special mini-chariots are also made of silver.

Utensils and objects used for rituals comprise an entire world of religion, beliefs and, above all, divine art, which has exerted its regional influences on utensils used in rituals from other parts of the country. Many have travelled far and have found places in some of the great museums of the world, where they can be admired for their sheer beauty and craftsmanship.

MODERN INDIAN SILVER

Indian art and handicrafts have since time immemorial, captivated the imagination of people all over the world. Every Indian state boasts of exclusive crafts in textile, ivory, wood or metal. The rich craftsmanship varies depending on historical influences on the region, the patrons, existing hereditary skills, and available raw material. Like many Indian crafts, Indian silverware is well known for its special features, which change continually with time and the demands of the patrons and the market.

Ornaments, household utensils and utility objects in silver were popular in olden days among royalty, dignitaries and affluent families. The lure of silver has diminished little with time and young people often prefer antique-looking silver jewellery over heavy gold ornaments. Also, with a demand for corporate gifts, designers have a ready market for silver artefacts.

Dariba Kalan near Chandni Chowk, Delhi, is a hub for silver lovers. Nearly 150 shops, stretching over half a kilometre, sell silver jewellery and other silverware. Also known as Silver Street, Dariba Kalan is the oldest and largest silver market of Asia and has been referred to in Mughal records during Shahjahan's reign in the seventeenth century. Most shoppers look for antique jewellery, utility objects and coins depicting figures of Ganesha, Lakshmi or other deities. During Diwali and the festive season around October and November, there is the maximum sale of silver objects, including gift items like dinner- and tea-sets. Beautifully carved silver purses currently in fashion, weighing about 200 gm and priced between Rs 3,000 Rs 5,000, are also sold in some shops. An affordable range of silver earrings, chains and pendants in oxidized silver cater to the young crowd.

Facing Page:
Spherical decorative item with carefully crafted cutwork floral designs

Left:
Stately silver deep stambh *(oil lamp port) with diyas (containers for wax) placed on both sides of an ornate stand ornamented with silver pendents*

Facing Page:
Silver bells with deities forming the fancifully shaped handles

The oldest shop in Dariba Kalan is that of Ratan Chand Jwala Nath jewellers, in business since the eighteenth century. Some shopkeepers specialize in making silver trophies and medals. Trophies for distribution in schools and colleges as well as other artefacts are worked with etching or embossing techniques; motifs include deities, logos of institutes or other designs specified by clients. The increased number of competitions and the trend of distributing trophies and medals have given silver craft a new dimension. To further increase the demand for silverware, some silversmiths have tied up with the National Institute of Fashion Technology to give their designs a contemporary look.

Price plays an important role in the silver business. Since it is less expensive than gold, many people can afford silver. Items made with a combination of silver and semi-precious stones have helped make the silver market prosper. Jewellery pieces, images of deities and other decorative objects are popular. Affluent people and art lovers are partial to silver studded jewellery, which they wear for parties and weddings. Decorative pieces are in demand for drawing- and living-rooms and also as gifts and souvenirs. A large shop called Cooke & Kelvey, in Janpath, New Delhi, deals in a range of silverware. A branch of the original shop in Kolkata (West Bengal), which opened in

lamps, incense burners, incense storage pots and other utensils and items related to worship, images of gods and goddesses are also made and sold by the company. Bar accessories are widely used in modern society. The affluent have bars in their homes and prefer to have decorative objects to keep bottles on. Holding stands, bottle openers and cooling utensils are also made of silver in beautiful bird and animal shapes as well as objects shaped in the female form or made to look like dolls.

Other silver decorative objects much in demand are carved photo-frames, glittering night lamps with semi-precious stones, embedded candlestands with several wicks, various types of boxes for keeping jewellery and precious stones, silver ash-trays, and a variety of decorative bird and animal figures.

Silver craftmanship is thriving today in India. The silver filigree work of Cuttack, in Orissa, is renowned for its delicacy. Scent-holders, rosewater sprinklers, smoking pipes, trays, plates and drinking glasses are the utility items usually made, along with decorative items into human figures, such as dancers, and animals. Silver wire is beaten flat and joined according to desired patterns in such a way that joints are not easily visible. The prices of such objects are fixed according to the intricacy of the workmanship and the labour involved in making them.

Kashmir is famous for its parcel-gilded silverware. The pattern consists of small sprigs of leaves hammered out in relief all over the vessel. Known as the Ganga–Jamuna pattern, the background may be in silver and the sprigs in parcel gilt. The most popular object made in Kashmir is the samovar, a traditional item used for preparing *kahva* (spiced tea). Samovars are made of tin or silver and are sometimes gilded. Jammu and Kashmir also specialize in other traditional utensils, the most popular being the *surahi*, plates, goblets, cups and tea-pots, and jewellery made in silver. The designs of Kashmiri jewellery are inspired by landscapes, birds, fruit, leaves and flowers which are engraved on the ornament. Oxidized silver jewellery is also quite popular in Kashmir, especially in the Tibetan style.

Below:
Silver box in the realistic shape of a tortoise, ornamented with a grooved shell, 20th century

Facing Page:
Serving bowl in silver with a unique stand composed of four standing elephants, 20th century.

Facing Page:
Embellished with elaborately detailed work is this heavy silver statuette of Lord Ganesh in a seated pose, 20th century

Kashmiri silverware is of two main types, either plain or engraved. Each silver piece is handmade in a high quality of workmanship and fine finish. About 2,000 craftsmen are engaged in silver work in Kashmir. Due to its quality, Kashmiri silverware is in great demand worldwide, especially in the Middle East. In the Jammu area, Dogra silver jewellery is very popular, especially in rural areas. These rustic silver ornaments are heavy and used mostly by tribal people like the Gujjar, Bakewal and Gaddi women. Ladakh silverware is currently very popular, especially its beautiful jewellery and traditional formal silver cups and bowls. Kashmiri silversmiths make exquisite bracelets, earrings, ear-studs, necklace and bangles in silver. Ornaments studded with precious and semi-precious stones are popular among Kashmiris. Silver ornaments are also demand in Rajasthan, where the important centres of silver jewellery are Sahapura, Soni Pakrojji, Jaipur and Jodhpur. Among the most important centres of silver jewellery in Gujarat are Rajkot, Paddari, Bhuj and Jamnagar.

A few areas of Uttar Pradesh, such as Lucknow, Rampur, Moradabad and Mathura are the main centres of silverware. The articles produced include tea-sets, plates and saucers, sugar and milk pots, jewellery and decorative and religious objects, but the designs here are distinctive with some of the pieces in plain silver and some ornamental. Here, engraving and repoussé techniques are also used for ornamentation. In Lucknow, the main patterns depict hunting and jungle scenes or feature snake and *swamy* designs. Silver animal toys are made in Mathura.

Haryana has not had any royal patronage for this art, as a result of which more priority has been given to functional objects, with simple ornamentation. Rewari, Nuh, Bhiwani, Hissar and Rohtak in Haryana are better known for silver work, especially for their jewellery. Silversmiths in Nuh and Rewari have now started making chunky imitation silver jewellery for export and the urban market. Karnal produces characteristic hollow silver beads, Ambala excels in chiselled silver bracelets, and at Panipat one will find necklaces made of fine silver beads.

In Punjab, Amritsar, Patiala, Ludhiana, Kapurthala and some hilly areas are the main centres of silver arts. The Amritsar style is completely influenced by Kashmiri craftsmanship. Religious items like small temples, Shree Granth Sahib stands and fans are also produced in silver.

Maharashtra also produces a range of silver items. Mumbai, the biggest cosmopolitan city of India, is the forerunner in this field. Like Delhi and Kolkata, Mumbai also has a large number

Right:
Graceful candlestand made of silver, the unusual stand in the shape of a human figure holding the candlebra

of clients who are keen to purchase silver decorative objects, household utility and religious objects as well as jewellery. Hupri, near Kolhapur, is the forerunner in silver jewellery manufacturing in Maharashtra. It has 400 production units, and provides employment to 3,000 men on a regular basis and to over 1,000 women who work at home at their leisure hours. A separate piece of land outside the village has been developed where more than 250 residence-cum-workshop units function in Hupri, making silverware objects and jewellery. They supply silverware both to Mumbai and abroad.

Nasik is another important silverware centre in Maharashtra. Ritual objects are made here because Nasik is an important pilgrim centre for Hindus. Images of deities, *kumkum* (vermilion) boxes are most popular, but other attractive utility objects are also produced such as *paandaan* (betel box), *gulab-pash* (rose-water sprinkler), *itardaan* (scent bottle), bowls and trays. Kolhapur also manufactures similar silver objects.

A rich variety of silver jewellery is created in Rajasthan, to cover every part of the body. Each city has its distinctive style. Jaipur work is noted for its bulkiness with occasional grace of form. Jaipur craftsmen are experts in surface embellishment where they engrave figures realistically. They also make large scent-holders with numerous receptacles for perfume, arranged like buds on a tree, betel holders, rosewater sprinklers and other decorative and utility items. These silver items are plain but embossed and pierced in bold floral and geometrical designs. In Alwar, silversmiths make silver objects, including cups, saucers, tea-pots, *huqqas* and other decorative objects in filigree and chased work. Bikaner also produces silver work, including images of gods and goddess, temple shrines, trappings and ornaments of elephants and camels, apart from routine silverware.

In South India, silver articles are made in solid form, mostly as religious or utility items. Silver images of gods and goddess are sold in the markets, as are five-headed snake covers for Shiva *lingams*, lamps in candle-stick shapes, card cases, scent caskets, betel-nut boxes and silver shallow bowls. Silversmiths make objects in chased form with ornamentation, embossing and in filigree style. Jewellery is also made in South India, used mostly by Muslim women or in Muslim-influenced areas.

Small towns in India also produce silver utensils, religious items and jewellery for the middle class. On auspicious occasions, people gift these to relatives. The cheapest and most attractive items are jewellery, glasses, spoons, plates and bowls made of silver. Toe-rings are made of silver, as it is believed that wearing gold

Left:
Sleek lines of an elegant silver water jug with an exquisitely embellished surface

Left: *A silver temple and a* diya *(lamp) stand*

Facing Page:
On the curved rim of this flower-shaped pooja thali *(tray for religious items) are the* ashta mangalik *(eight deities), ornamenting each gold-polished petal shape*

toe-rings is inauspicious for the user, which is why even affluent women wear silver ones.

Silver is extensively used in India even though its production does not really meet the demand. This is the reason why India has imported silver from foreign countries, to make jewellery and other items. Napkin rings and powder-boxes made with motifs drawn from Hindu mythology and then encrusted in silver, against finely engraved backgrounds, exemplify both superlative skill and mastery of material.

The best quality of Indian silversmiths is that they make artefacts using their traditional skills and values, while innovating always, exhibiting the flexibility of making changes according to the needs of their customers. The changed scenario of clientele from royalty to the common man has given silversmiths and designers new vistas, much wider than that of the past. Today, in the global village, they work with more challenges facing them, but have been able to meet new dimensions of modernity while practising in the rich traditions of their age-old craft.

GLOSSARY

Aftaba	Wine dispenser with a long spout
Bajuband	Armlet
Bichhua	Toe-ring worn by women as a sign of wedlock
Bidri work	Mixed metal work which results in a dull black colour with an inlayed silver pattern. It gets its name from from Bidar, a place in Karnataka, where t his workmanship originated
Ganga–Jamuna	A combination of two metals or two colours. It is named after two great rivers of India: Ganga symbolizes gold and Jamuna represents silver
Hansuli	A solid silver or gold collar
Haathphool	A hand ornament
Hauda	A seat on an elephant's back
Huqqa	A tobacco pipe with a long, flexible tube, which draws the smoke through water contained in a bowl
Itardaan	A small jar for perfumes
Jhumka	A pair of dangling earrings
Kalash	A container for sacred water in the temples
Kara	Thick bangles
Karanphool	A pair of heavy earrings
Koftagiri	Gold and silver inlay work
Laung	A small nose-ring in the shape of a clove
Lota	A small, rounded water pot
Nath	A nose-ring
Paizeb	A type of anklet.
Pan kanta	Hair ornament of Bengal
Paunchi	Strung silver beads in the shape of flower buds
Phuli	A small nose-ring
Shilpashastra	Science of architecture/handicrafts
Sindoordaani	Vermilion powder container
Surahi	A water jar with a long spout
Tara kanta	A local name for hair ornaments in Bengal
Thali	Black beads and silver or gold necklace worn by Indian ladies as sign of wedlock
Tika	A flat pendant suspended over the forehead
Zar nishan	Shallow inlay work in gold or silver

BIBLIOGRAPHY

Brijbhushan, Dr. Jamila, *Masterpieces of Indian Jewellery* Taraporewala Publications, Mumbai, 1979

Chandra, Rai Govind, *Indo-Greek Jewellery,* Abhinava Publications, New Delhi, 1979

Chandra, Rai Govind, *Studies in the Development of Ornaments and Jewellery in Proto-Historic India,* 1964

Chattopadhyay, Kamala Devi, *The Glory of Indian Handicrafts* Indian Book Company, New Delhi, 1976

Chattopadhyay, Kamala Devi, *Indian Handicrafts,* Allied Publications, New Delhi, 1963

Chattopadhyay, Kamala Devi, *Handicrafts of India,* New Age International Publishers Ltd., New Delhi, 1995.

Dhamija, Ram, *Sixty Years of Writing on Arts and Crafts in India,* Sterling Publications, New Delhi, 1988

Dhamija, Jasleen, *Indian Folk Arts and Crafts,* National Book House, New Delhi, 1970

Gupta, Dr. Parameshwari Lal, *Coins,* National Book Trust, New Delhi, 1996

Govind, Dr. Vijay, *The growth of science & technology as gleaned from the classical account of India,* an article published in the Journal of Indian History, New Delhi

Handley, Thomas Holbeign, *Indian Jewellery, Low Price Publications,* Delhi, 1991/93

Jain-Neubaur, Dr. Juta, *Chandrka, Silver Ornaments of India,* Timeless Books, New Delhi, 2001

Jain-Neubaur, Dr. Juta, *Feet and Footwear in Indian Culture,* Bata Shoe Museum Foundation, Canada, 2000

Jha, Dr. Amateshwar, *Bharatiya Sikka, Ek Aitihasik Parichaya,* Indian Institute of Research in Numismatic Studies, Ajneri, Nasik, Maharashtra, 2003

Kimberley Mastelle & Jeffery B. Spurr, *Silver and Shawls,* an article published in Harvard University, Art Museum Gallery Series No. 46, 2000

Lal Krishna, *Bidariware,* National Museum, New Delhi, 1990

Mahapatra, Ram Prasad, *Ornaments of Orissa,* B.R. Publication Corporation, Delhi, 1981

Mathur, Dr. Asha Rani, *A Jewelled Splendour: The Tradition of Indian Jewellery,* Rupa & Co., New Delhi, 2002

Nandgopal, Dr. Chudamani and Vatsala Ayengar, *Temple Treasures,* Vol. 1 & 2 Craft Council of Karnataka, Bangalore, 1995

Nigam, Dr. M. Lal, *Indian Jewellery,* Lustre Press, Roli Books, New Delhi, 1999

Mukherjee, T.N., *Art Manufactures of India,* Aryan Books International, Delhi, 2000

Saraf, D.N., *Indian Crafts, Developments & Potential,* Vikash Publishing House Pvt. Ltd., Delhi

Strong, Susan, *The Jewels of India,* Marg Publication, Mumbai, 1980

Untrachtt, Oppi, *Traditional Jewellery of India,* Thames and Hudson, London, 1997

Vanaja, R., *Indian Coinage, National Museum,* New Delhi

ACKNOWLEDGEMENTS

I am thankful to Dr A.K.V.S. Reddy, Director-General of the National Museum, New Delhi and Mr U. Das, Director (Administration and Collection) of the National Museum, for allowing me to work on this project and source photographs from the National Museum collection.

The project could not have been completed without the support of Dr Rita Sharma, Curator (Numismatics and Epigraphy), Ms Jayshree Sharma, Curator (Anthropology), and Ms Anju Sachdeva, Assistant Curator (Anthropology). I am also thankful to my friend Dr Naval Krishna, Joint Director, Bharat Kala Bhavan, Varanasi, for his guidance.

I also thank Ms Pratibha Prashar, Senior Librarian, and her staff at the National Museum Library; the staff of the American Library in Gurgaon; Mr J.C.Arora, former photographic officer, and Mr Tejbir Singh, photo officer, of the National Museum, New Delhi; and Mr Dharmendra. Special thanks to Mr T.S. Chatterjee, Manager, Cooke and Kelvey, Janpath, New Delhi, for sharing his knowledge on modern silver objects and to photographer Dheeraj Paul for photographing these objects.

Thanks also to my mother-in-law Urmila Dwivedi, son Neelabh, daughter Anvita, nephew Abhishek and the rest of my family for their deep interest in the completion of this project. Last but not the least, my deep sense of gratitude to my wife, Anamika Pathak, for her unconditional support and cooperation in the completion of this book.

PHOTO CREDITS

All photographs/illustrations from the National Museum,
New Delhi, except those listed below:
Roli Books: 104, 114
Dheeraj Paul (courtesy Cooke & Kelvey, New Delhi): 11, 120, 122,
123, 126, 127, 129, 130, 131, 132, 133
Prakash Israni: 28 (third from top), 30, 83